insight text guide

Scott Hurley

The Freedom of the City

Brian Friel

First published in 2001, reprinted with revisions in 2015.

Insight Publications Pty Ltd
3/350 Charman Road
Cheltenham VIC 3192
Australia
Tel: +61 3 8571 4950
Fax: +61 3 8571 0257
Email: books@insightpublications.com.au

www.insightpublications.com.au

ISBN: 9781875882663 (paperback)

Acknowledgement
The author and the publishers thank Ross Huggard for reference material and notes used as resource materials in the development of this text guide.

Cover design: The Modern Art Production Group

Printed in Australia

contents

CHARACTER MAP

Commentators

The Priest
Administers last rites and celebrates requiem Mass for the trio; sees their lives as a sacrifice.

The Balladeer
Sings songs that celebrate Irish heroes; shows how myths can develop around ordinary individuals.

Dr Dodds
American professor of sociology; has specialist area 'the subculture of poverty'. Speaks at length at critical points but does not interact with any other characters.

Liam O'Kelly
Television news reporter; gives information and misinformation that play a role in the deaths of the three protagonists.

Army Press Officer
Gives press release that reconstructs trio as 'terrorists'; refuses to answer questions that would implicate the army.

Trio in Mayor's parlour

Skinner
(Adrian Casimir Fitzgerald) Single, unemployed, 21 years old, no living relatives traced, no fixed address. In trouble with the law for minor offences but not a known 'terrorist'.

Lily
(Elizabeth M Doherty) Married, mother of 11 children, 43 years old, housewife and occasional cleaning woman.

Michael
(Michael Joseph Hegarty) Single, unemployed, 22 years old. Lives with his parents; engaged; studying business, economics & computer science to improve himself.

Outside the Guildhall

The Soldiers
Report that protesters have entered the Mayor's parlour; remove the three bodies after the shooting.

Tribunal of inquiry

The Judge
English, early 60s, appointed by British Government, former Army man.

The Policeman
First witness before Tribunal; gives important background information about the trio.

Brigadier Johnson-Hansbury
In charge of security; claims the 'terrorists' emerged firing so it was impossible to arrest them.

Dr Winbourne
A Scotsman from the Army Forensic Department; gives evidence about lead particles on the bodies of the deceased.

Professor Cuppley
Pathologist who carried out the post-mortem examinations. Testifies to the gruesome injuries inflicted by high-velocity rifle fire.

INTRODUCTION

Brian Friel was born in 1929 in Omagh, Northern Ireland, of a Catholic family. When he was ten they moved to Derry (as it is called by Catholics – its official name is Londonderry). Friel studied to become a priest in Maynooth, Ireland, but decided against taking orders. He returned to Northern Ireland and became a schoolteacher in Derry for ten years. In 1960 he left teaching to write full time. He has published many short stories, but he is most famous for his plays. Friel is considered to be Ireland's leading playwright – he is the author of more than a dozen original plays and has also written numerous adaptations of plays by writers such as Chekhov and Turgenev, transposing already existing English translations into Irish settings. His masterpieces are *Translations* (1980) and *Dancing at Lughnasa* (1990). He has lived in Donegal in the Republic of Ireland since the late 1960s.

The Freedom of the City (1973) opened first at the Abbey Theatre in Dublin, with international openings soon after. A highly political play, it met harsh criticism in New York and London. During a period of violent unrest sharpened by the events of 'Bloody Sunday', the play was viewed by some as an apology (if not outright propaganda) for the IRA (Irish Republican Army) who were at that time engaging in terrorist activities against the British in Northern Ireland.

This play revolves around the imaginary shooting by British soldiers of three civil rights demonstrators. The demonstrators have inadvertently sought shelter in the Mayor's parlour of the Guildhall in Derry after security forces break up a mass demonstration using tear gas and rubber bullets. The play simultaneously presents their last hours as well as the British inquiry conducted after the event. It tensely builds towards a climax equating the murders with the findings of the inquiry.

BACKGROUND & CONTEXT

In order to understand the political aspects of *The Freedom of the City*, it is necessary to understand some basics of the history of Northern Ireland.

A brief history of Northern Ireland

The ancient nation of Ireland has been divided into two different countries, the Republic of Ireland in the south and Northern Ireland in the north, since 1922. The Republic of Ireland is composed of all but six of the island's more than thirty counties; the remaining six (in the region called Ulster) became the separate nation of Northern Ireland. The Republic of Ireland is Catholic and Northern Ireland is Protestant, though many Catholics do still live in the latter. Northern Ireland is a member of the United Kingdom, and due to civil strife it has been ruled by England since 1972. The violence that has been recurring in Northern Ireland since the 1960s, often referred to as 'the Troubles', has pitted Catholic forces (Nationalists/Republicans), who want to reunite the country with the Republic of Ireland, against Protestant forces (Unionists/Loyalists), who want it to remain part of the United Kingdom. This is an issue that has not yet been resolved.

Protestants encouraged to settle in Northern Ireland

Why was Ireland partitioned in this way? In the sixteenth century, in order to maintain dominance over the island, the British tried to encourage the movement of British and Scottish settlers to these six counties of Ulster. These migrants, under the auspices of the British colonising forces, prospered and grew into a substantial community of Protestants in a sea of Catholicism – the religion of the rest of Ireland. The Protestant migrants and their descendants were divided into two classes: a wealthy class of landholding farmers and a yeomen class who worked for them. This left the native Catholics in the region of Ulster landless, with only the most menial and unpromising occupations.

Protestant–Catholic conflict

Bitterness between Protestants and Catholics in Northern Ireland has flared up in events of sectarian violence since the 1600s. In 1798 an Irish rebellion, initiated by Wolfe Tone, was brutally put down by the British (more than 35,000 lives were lost on both sides). This led to the Act of Union in 1800 disbanding the fledgling Irish Parliament and taking away any autonomy the nation had. In 1886 British Prime Minister Gladstone introduced the First Home Rule Bill to the Parliament, but it was defeated. In 1912 Home Rule for Ireland was finally approved, but as war clouds gathered, implementation was put off until after what turned out to be World War I.

The 1916 Easter Uprising in Dublin brought matters to a head. It was suppressed by the British and its leaders executed – popular heroes Patrick Pearce and James Connolly among them. The newly formed IRA (Irish Republican Army) was waging war on the 'Black and Tans' (British soldiers), and Protestant forces were gathering in Ulster for all-out civil war between themselves and Catholics in the south if the British pulled out of Ulster completely. Against this backdrop of great violence and unrest, the Anglo-Irish treaty was signed – so it was that twenty-six counties became the Republic of Ireland and six became the nation of Northern Ireland.

The civil rights movement in Northern Ireland

Northern Ireland is governed by a parliamentary system. Since the Anglo-Irish treaty, Protestants (the Unionist party) have always been in the majority and Catholics (the Nationalist party) have been in opposition. There were decades of utter domination by ruling Protestant governments. Catholics withdrew from the political process almost entirely until the

1960s when, encouraged by the remarkable gains made by African-Americans in the United States, they formed a civil rights movement.

The first major event of this movement was the 5 October 1968 march (mentioned by Michael in the play). It was organised in Derry by the Derry Housing Action Committee and the Northern Ireland Civil Rights Association (NICRA). Before it properly began, the march was broken up by Northern Ireland's police force, the Royal Ulster Constabulary (RUC). The next few years saw many such marches and demonstrations organised by NICRA. The civil rights movement coincided with a rebirth of the IRA, dormant since the 1930s. They began agitating, often violently, for reunification with the Republic of Ireland.

Things soon got out of hand. Groups of Protestant paramilitary groups began forming; they and the IRA exchanged bullets and bombs. Many were killed. The IRA itself broke into two separate groups: the traditional IRA who quit violence and were guided by Marxist political theories; and the Provisional IRA. The latter group committed themselves to violence against the Orange (Protestant) paramilitaries, against the RUC and against Britain itself, which sent forces of its army into Northern Ireland in 1971. Amid this violence the NICRA continued conducting nonviolent civil rights protests.

Bloody Sunday

A major NICRA nonviolent event took place on 30 January 1972 – a march in Derry protesting against the government policy of 'internment' (the arresting and holding of suspected Catholic agitators without trial). The events surrounding Bloody Sunday are of utmost importance to *The Freedom of the City* because the play is based on a fictional occurrence that parallels the Bloody Sunday events in many ways.

The facts of Bloody Sunday – January 1972

During the protest march – which had been banned by the authorities – soldiers from the elite British Parachute Regiment were ordered to make arrests of some youths in the Bogside area who had thrown rocks. They began firing live rounds into the crowd. Half an hour later, thirteen protesters had been killed and thirteen others had been wounded (a fourteenth victim died in June of that year). After the event, paratroopers claimed, first, that they had come under gunfire and bomb attack from IRA fighters, and second, that they had only shot people who carried weapons. Testimony from eyewitnesses directly refutes this, averring that none of the dead had been armed. An inquiry was held weeks later led by the British Chief Lord Justice, Lord Widgery. The soldiers' claims were upheld, but controversy has lived on with the insistence that the soldiers killed unarmed civilians.

Key point

Most notorious among the inquest's actions was its concentration on the presence of lead powder on some of the victims. Lord Widgery concluded that at least some of the victims had fired or were near people who had fired; in this he ignored testimony given by forensic experts that the bodies could have been contaminated by the soldiers who handled them. Also ignored or dismissed was evidence suggesting that at least one of the victims had his hands raised above his head when shot and that at least one had been shot in the back while lying prone. The inquest became known by some as the 'Widgery Whitewash'.

Bloody Sunday riveted the attention of the world, leading eventually to a suspension of the powers of the Northern Irish government. While many had died in 'the Troubles' before that day and many innocents were to die afterwards in horrific circumstances (for example, in the bombings in Enniskillen and Omagh), Bloody Sunday was the first time that British troops had opened fire on protesters. The killings were thus seen as a part of 'policy' rather than acts of sectarian violence. The Widgery findings only added fuel to the fire; the way that they tended to blame the victims has been seen as an official justification of murder by the British government.

New inquiry

In 1998 the Blair Government in London announced that a new inquiry was to be conducted into the events of Bloody Sunday. This inquiry revealed frightening evidence that suggests once again that the Widgery Inquiry was little more than an official cover-up of the actions of the military. One paratrooper has testified that his lieutenant told his troops the day before, 'We want some kills tomorrow.' He claims that a soldier fired on a group of civilians from about five metres, killing one and wounding a bystander whom he then killed. The paratrooper also stated that when the crowd saw the heavily armed troops walking towards them, they stopped and raised their hands above their heads.

It is important to remember that, as critics have noted, Brian Friel is not recreating Bloody Sunday but responding to Lord Widgery's official inquiry.

The setting – time and place

Friel sets *The Freedom of the City* in February 1970, two years before Bloody Sunday. Yet some aspects of 1972 are paralleled throughout the play. An audience at the premier in Dublin would have recognised the significance of the Judge's inquiry in the play and its testimony on lead smears; they would have recognised the comments and manner of Lord Widgery in the Judge. And the final image of Skinner, Lily and Michael holding their hands above their heads would have been likewise fraught with meaning.

Derry (also known as Londonderry) has long been a site of contention – even its name is still debated. Generally Catholics/Nationalists favour using the name *Derry*, while Protestants/Unionists use *Londonderry*. In 1925 the Boundary Commission kept the city in Northern Ireland to the great disappointment of the Catholics. One consequence for the Catholic population was a housing policy that restricted them to the tenancies in very overcrowded South Ward; another was that the city's Magee College missed out on becoming a university. This meant that the growing Catholic population became increasingly frustrated and angry. Tensions exploded into conflicts on 5 October 1968, the 'Battle of the Bogside' (August 1969) and Bloody Sunday (1972). By the 1990s Derry was popularly described as a city divided by the river into 'east bank' (Protestant) and 'west bank' (Catholic). A more stable environment brought some improvements evident in a major expansion of Magee College, better housing and increased investment.

GENRE, STYLE & STRUCTURE

The Freedom of the City is, of course, a play; though we may enjoy reading it as a text, bear in mind that it was written by Brian Friel to be performed.

While Friel does give some instructions about the personalities and appearances of his main characters, and he gives required stage directions, there is plenty of room for interpretation. As you read the play, think about how the roles should be performed, considering how much the characters reveal (or conceal) themselves in their words.

Structure: two narrative strands

Let's look at some of the challenging aspects to the structure of this play. There are two main narrative strands; they could almost be thought of as sub-plays. The first revolves around the court of inquiry conducted by the Judge (Strand A). The second involves the last hours of the protagonists (Strand B). The play opens with the simultaneous performance of the first scene in the court inquiry (Strand A) and the very last scene in the lives of the main characters (Strand B). The Judge opens his inquiry by interviewing the Policeman (weeks after the killing, presumably) as the bodies of Skinner, Lily and Michael are being dragged away moments after their murder. From here things get a little easier. Strand A continues without detouring from the chronological order of the inquiry. Strand B doubles back to the beginning of the story of the three characters and then proceeds chronologically, working its way to that gripping moment with which it began. Strand A ends with the Judge's conclusion; Strand B ends with the shootings.

Other important features of structure

There are further features to be noted. Some scenes, such as the speeches of the Priest, are not attached directly to Strand A or to Strand B. These scenes do not necessarily occur chronologically. For instance, in Act One there is a cluster of three scenes – the Priest's first address; some Voices outside the Guildhall; and a news conference – that take place (respectively) a day or two after the killings; immediately after the killings; and hours before the killings. Chronology is subverted, but not without reason. These scenes are linked thematically; they each involve characters commenting on the central events of the play in very different ways. Friel forces us to account for such differences by placing these scenes together.

Style: Friel's 'metatheatre'

'Metatheatre' is theatre that calls attention to itself as theatre – that is, it uses devices that make the audience aware that they are in the theatre.

In *The Freedom of the City* there are some scenes that take place *outside* any discernible chronology. These are the speeches by Dr Dodds and the speeches made by Skinner, Lily and Michael early in Act Two concerning the moment of their deaths.

Dr Dodds does not take any hand in the action. His comments on the 'subculture of poverty' are not testimony of the tribunal, nor are they specifically attached to the events of the play in any way. He is simply introduced and dismissed because what he has to say may be relevant to the action we see. Friel is engaging in a practice called 'metatheatre', bending, if not breaking, the 'rules' of theatre. One rule of traditional theatre would demand Dr Dodds' speeches to be spoken by one of the characters 'within' the story. It is not 'believable' or consistent that Dr Dodds should just appear and disappear out of nowhere when the time and circumstances of all the other characters are accounted for.

Concerning the speeches in Act Two by Skinner, Lily and Michael, the rules broken are obvious. How can people speak about their own deaths? Even if they were not dead, they should not be speaking directly to *us*, should they? As the audience we observe action played out before us. To address us is basically to initiate conversation and thus draw us into the action.

The fourth wall of theatre

One of the foundational 'rules' of theatre concerns something called the 'fourth wall'. This means that characters are not supposed to behave as though they *know* there is an audience watching them. Beyond the proscenium arch (that is, beyond the stage) is not an auditorium full of people, but just another wall in the room where the scene has been set.

These speeches, by Dodds and the three protagonists, break down that fourth wall. They take away the 'believability' of the play. An audience agrees, whether it realises it or not, to 'suspend disbelief'. That's a literary way of saying that for the sake of being able to enjoy the play, the audience agrees to believe that we have been allowed to silently observe a 'real' story. When a play breaks down the fourth wall, the agreement between play and audience is broken. The play, shouting, 'I'm a play', loses that aura of 'believability' and the audience is forced to see it for what it is. Metatheatre, then, is simply theatre that calls attention to itself as theatre.

Why does Friel use it? Well, he is by no means the first. Metatheatre was one of the staples of twentieth-century drama. Some of its most notable proponents are Luigi Pirandello and Bertolt Brecht. Brecht developed a concept called Epic Theatre. In a nutshell, he wanted to break audiences and playwrights out of the rut of believability. He employed something called in German *verfremdungseffekt*, or 'alienation effect', achieved by any kind of theatrical device that breaks the illusion of reality for the spectator (the players might break into song, for instance, during a poignant moment). Behind this is a political motive.

The ancient Greek philosopher Aristotle, in the *Poetics*, wrote on the cathartic effect of theatre. We watch actors plumb the depths of human emotion and tragedy; observing it we feel enlightened or purged. We 'connect' with it, but only because we are detached *from* it. Brecht wanted a theatre without the kind of catharsis that makes us identify with individuals who are helplessly subject to their fate; he wanted a theatre based on the kind of scientific detachment that motivates people to *act* on political issues rather than merely observe. By breaking down the fourth wall, Epic Theatre alienates the audience from the Aristotelian norm. Instead of watching a play and disappearing into the world shown to us (shedding a tear perhaps and then going out and having a good meal when it's all over), Brecht wants us to be detached. He wants us to look at social problems and then go out and do something about them.

This is by no means the extent of Epic Theatre, nor does Friel follow most of Brecht's prescriptions. *The Freedom of the City* is far too dramatic to be considered truly Brechtian. Yet it could be argued that the reason Friel engages in *verfremdungseffekt* in the scenes mentioned is indeed Brechtian.

Key point

The playwright wants to snap us out of viewing these characters as contained by their circumstances, as tragic figures 'different' from the audience. Skinner, Lily and Michael are members of a broader movement with which Friel encourages the audience to identify and take action. Breaking the fourth wall can help to do that.

SCENE-BY-SCENE ANALYSIS

NOTE: There are no formal scenes in this two-act play. For purposes of study, sections within each act have been numbered as scenes and page referenced.

ACT ONE

Opening (p.107)

The play opens to a very disturbing scene: '*Three bodies lie grotesquely across the front of the stage*'. Friel's startling opening ensures the immediate interest of the audience and promises that this play is not going to be frivolous or lightweight. It will challenge us.

The opening, when read, can be rather confusing. If we were actually seeing this play rather than reading it, we'd realise quite quickly that we are seeing two separate scenes occurring at different times but enacted together on the one stage. The first scene, occurring without dialogue, involves the last rites being given to the three bodies by the Priest and their removal by the nervous soldiers, conducted at the front of the stage. The second scene occurs perhaps many days later; it shows the Judge overseeing a judicial inquiry into the deaths of the three persons who are identified as Skinner, Lily and Michael. This occurs on a different part of the stage.

These scenes may be occurring at different dramatic times and places, but of course they are related. Notice the clever technique Friel uses not only to identify the three main characters, but also to 'link' the two scenes: as the Policeman reads the name and occupation of one of the dead to the Judge in the court, the Priest gives that character his or her last rites downstage. Only theatre can use this kind of technique, called *juxtaposition*, with such ease and success.

Scene 1 (pp.107–10)

Summary: *The inquiry begins with the Judge interviewing the Policeman.*

Key point

This scene initiates the central question of the inquiry: were the three armed and did they fire at the soldiers before being killed?

The Judge asks the Policeman about the presence of firearms on or near the bodies of Skinner, Lily and Michael. The latter qualifies his answer, saying that he saw none, but that he was not the first to come upon them. It is only when the Judge finishes questioning the Policeman and turns to address his courtroom that the audience can fully understand the setting from which he speaks. He explains the nature of the court of inquiry, stressing that it is a 'fact-finding exercise' meant to form 'an objective view of the events' (p.109) surrounding the deaths of the three main characters. These words echo the terms used by Lord Widgery to open the inquest following Bloody Sunday.

Friel takes this opportunity to set the scene: Skinner, Lily and Michael were killed following a civil rights rally in the city of Derry in February, 1970, after they had occupied a municipal building (the Mayor's parlour of the Guildhall). We should remember the Judge's words about objectivity when we assess his summation of the proceedings (p.168) at the end of the play.

Scene 2 (pp.110–11)

Summary: *Dr Dodds' first speech about 'the subculture of poverty'; also introduces concepts of 'objectivity'.*

An American professor of sociology addresses the audience as though giving a lecture at a conference. He is not a witness in the inquiry, but a kind of spokesperson, possibly for the playwright. We need to be careful, however, about concluding whether this character truly represents Brian Friel's beliefs (see 'Characters & Relationships', p.39).

Dodds' subject is the 'subculture of poverty', a way of living and thinking conditioned by extreme poverty, or 'the method [the poor] have devised to cope with the hopelessness and despair they experience because they know they'll never be successful in terms of the values and goals of the dominant society' (p.110). In other words, any capitalist society is based on the acquiring of money and material goods. Society smiles upon those able to do it and shuns those who cannot. Besides having to deal with the practical problems of poverty (food, shelter and the basic requirements of living), the poor live in a world constantly judging them as inadequate. Dodds tells us that the poor are 'provincial ... They know only their own troubles ... their own way of life' (p.111). The only way they can break out of this mentality is to realise that their problems are shared by millions of others around the world. This is what Dodds means by 'an objective view of their condition' (p.111). Once people are able to see beyond their local environment, they become politically aware, and with that often comes a political activity driven by anger and solidarity – and by hope. Our trio of characters exists in such extreme poverty, and they are obviously politically active. It will be up to us as we progress in the play to decide whether Dodds' thesis applies to them.

Key point

Note Friel's juxtaposition here: as Dr Dodds speaks to his imaginary audience, in the background, a woman is addressing the political rally just as troops are about to move in to break it up. We cannot hear her words, but we know they must be very politically charged. (See stage directions, p.110.)

Q By putting the two together, the Professor 'speaking over' the activist, is Friel telling us that even the words of someone as ostensibly 'objective' as the social scientist are political?

Scene 3 (pp.112–16)

Summary: *Skinner, Lily and Michael enter the Mayor's parlour; their contrasting characters are quickly apparent.*

After troops break up the demonstration, the three main characters find their way into the Mayor's parlour of the Guildhall. Skinner helps the other two who are blinded temporarily by CS gas.

They discuss the violent end to the rally, and even in the first pages of dialogue their personalities begin to show. Within a matter of moments Lily has told at least four funny anecdotes and is full of motherly advice for Michael who has been badly affected by the gas. Skinner is full of cutting remarks and sarcasm, but he really shows himself upon discovering that the trio has found its way into the Mayor's rooms – he laughs and somersaults and makes them guess where they are (pp.115–16).

Key point

The significance of the Mayor's parlour should be pointed out. Seeing themselves as subjected people, the three, but Skinner in particular, would consider 'His Worship, the Lord Mayor of Derry' (p.116), the representative of the English Crown to this city of Northern Ireland, as the absolute figurehead for everything they are fighting against. They have accidentally stumbled their way into the very lair of the enemy!

Scene 4 (pp.117–19)

Summary: *Outside the Guildhall: two soldiers, Liam O'Kelly, the Balladeer. These two short scenes show how quickly things can get out of hand.*

The dialogue of two soldiers (over their radios) outside the Guildhall tells us that the three have not gone unnoticed. Immediately following, Liam O'Kelly makes his report for his television network in Dublin (note that O'Kelly does not report for a Northern Irish agency), misrepresenting the number of people in the building – three unarmed civilians running blindly from conflict quickly become 'fifty armed gunmen' (p.117).

A crisis soon develops as people from the Bogside region (the Catholic slums, a hotbed for the protest movement) come to witness what one of them apparently calls 'the fall of the Bastille' (p.118). This refers to the opening event of the French Revolution, the storming on 14 July 1789 of the Bastille, the symbol to French commoners of the oppression of the aristocracy. The symbolic importance of the occupation of the Guildhall is not lost on O'Kelly, nor will it be on the army.

Significance of the Balladeer

A Balladeer enters and sings a song of defiance. He is obviously a representative of that part of the protest movement intent on reunifying north and south. More generally, this character symbolises the desire, crucial to political movements, for making heroes. Yet this goes beyond mere politics. Much of the Irish national identity has become associated with the element of resistance to the British. The Balladeer is trying to make the 'hundred Irish heroes' in the Guildhall – notice how the number keeps growing – into cultural icons like 'Tone, Pearce and Connolly' (p.118; also see 'Background & Context', p.3 in this Text Guide). This conflict has rapidly escalated into one pitting foreign guns against legend and cultural identity. Skinner, Lily and Michael are caught in the middle.

Scene 5 (pp.119–24)

Summary: *The trio explores the Mayor's parlour; Lily's history.*

Unaware of the crisis developing outside, the three explore their surroundings. Michael, who has said little to this point, is awe-struck. He uses words like 'beautiful' and 'impressive'. Skinner is flippant from the start, cracking jokes to show that unlike Michael he is clearly unimpressed:

> MICHAEL: Wardrobes – toilet – wash-hand basin – shower. Pink and black tiles all round. And the taps are gold and made like fishes' heads. God, it's very impressive. Isn't it impressive, Missus?

SKINNER: Isn't it, Missus?

LILY: It's all right.

SKINNER: Two pounds deposit against breakages and it's yours for ten bob a week. Or maybe you don't like the locality, Missus? (p.120)

Attitudes towards ruling authorities and characters' backgrounds

At first Lily is cautious, saying 'we shouldn't be here' (p.119), but she is soon imagining how she would change the place with glossy pink walls and brass duck ornaments. As we get to know these characters better we might notice parallels between their attitudes towards the place itself and towards the ruling order that normally occupies it. Skinner is flippant and cynical about the ruling elite; Michael is awed but believes that they can be reasoned with. For Lily, political attitudes manifest themselves as personal statements.

After examining the parlour, the three turn to getting to know each other. Michael is unemployed but is eager to work. In the interim he is taking classes at the technical institute to 'improve' himself. Clearly he is not subject to Dodds' 'hopelessness'. Lily is the mother of eleven children and the sole means of support to her family. Her husband, ironically nicknamed 'the chairman', is unable to work due, it would seem, to tuberculosis; he sits in his chair by the fire all day while Lily cleans houses. Lily is voluble; unlike the men who are a bit guarded, she is very open about her entire life.

Scene 6 (pp.124–7)

Summary: *The Priest's first speech, some Voices outside the Guildhall and a news conference.*

A few days after the events, the Priest addresses his congregation telling them about the requiem Mass to be celebrated for the three on the following morning. It is a moving speech, and quite political. The Priest insists that the three were martyrs to the cause of removing the 'iniquitous yoke' (p.125) upon them all. He sees their deaths as a call to action, one he hopes his parishioners will follow.

Following is a brief scene that goes back in time to immediately after the deaths of Skinner, Lily and Michael. It is the Voices of nameless people in the crowd conjecturing upon the aftermath of the killings. Again, we witness the exaggeration that seems naturally to accompany crisis situations: 'There's at least a dozen dead'; 'I heard fifteen or sixteen'; 'Maybe twenty' (p.125). Such exaggeration fuels the flames of resentment even higher; it is a kind of release of that resentment, almost an act of violence itself: 'Fuck them anyway! Fuck them! Fuck them!' (p.125).

This emotion contrasts with the business-like attitude presented by an officer giving a press conference. There has been a further step back in time – the scene occurs *while* the trio is still in the Guildhall. The Officer will not commit to anything and his language is devoid of emotion and individuality. When a press reporter asks if the insurgents in the Guildhall are armed he responds: 'Our information is that they have access to arms' (p.126). Significantly, this implies that, yes, they're armed, but it says it without taking responsibility for *actually* saying so.

Key point

In each of these three 'mini-scenes' we witness different types of rhetoric: the controlled but inspired pulpit speech of the Priest, the anguished and angry exaggeration of the crowd, and the deliberate officiousness of the Officer. The last is as much a piece of political rhetoric as the others; it shows the world that no human element will be allowed to sneak into the army's treatment of those it sees as terrorists. By juxtaposing these scenes, Friel is showing us just how wide the gulf is between the opposing sides on this issue and all those surrounding 'the Troubles' in Northern Ireland.

Scene 7 (127–32)

Summary: *Back in the parlour: Michael's politics and Skinner's history.*

Commenting on the size of the day's rally, Michael begins to reveal a bit of himself and his ideas on the 'cause'. He has been to all the rallies since the first on 5 October 1968, but he worries they are beginning to lose some of their dignity as they are infiltrated by what he calls the 'hooligan element', those who are looking more for mischief than civil rights. He is an idealist who believes that ordered, disciplined and dignified protest will eventually win respect and concessions from their rulers: 'And that's what we must show them – that we're responsible and respectable; and they'll come to respect what we're campaigning for' (pp.128–9). Skinner is quite dismissive about Michael's talk. At one point he mimics Michael's rhetoric without Michael realising he is being made fun of:

> MICHAEL: ... The ultimate objectives we're all striving for is more important than the personalities or the politics of the individuals concerned.
> SKINNER: At this point in time.
> MICHAEL: What's that?
> SKINNER: And taking full cognizance of all relative facts.
> MICHAEL: What d'you mean? (p.127)

When it comes to politics Michael tends to speak in cliches. Skinner only mildly teases here, but a little later he seems to really lose his temper. Michael reminisces about the early marches, with 'all those people marching along in silence, rich and poor, high and low, doctors, accountants, plumbers, teachers, bricklayers – all shoulder to shoulder' (p.129). It is one thing to speak in cliches, but quite another to think in them. While it is not announced what makes Skinner react so strongly, we will come to realise that for Skinner the struggle is one of class. He seems to believe that Michael is deluding himself in thinking that 'the high and low' (p.129) can really be together working for the same thing; it is the high who are keeping the low 'low'.

Skinner's history

Skinner uses the Mayor's telephone to make a bet on a horse race being run that afternoon. This prompts Lily to ask him some questions about his life. We learn that his parents died when he was a baby. He has worked, but not very recently or for any length of time. He obviously lives on his wits as we have learned from the Policeman's report in the first scene that he has 'no fixed address' (p.109). We have no idea what other forms his opportunism might take, though we know already (also from the Policeman's report) that he has been in trouble with the law on many occasions. He is definitely a member of Dr Dodds' subculture of poverty, a person for whom merely surviving is a constant struggle. That struggle seems to colour every part of Skinner's life – though we have much more to learn about him.

Michael's view of Skinner

Michael sees Skinner as a troublemaker and wonders if he is a 'revolutionary'. By this he means a communist, one who would change the discourse of Michael's civil rights protest to that of class struggle. This is really the crux of the budding distrust between Skinner and Michael. Michael believes quite strongly in capitalism; the trappings of wealth associated with the rulers of Derry awe him. He wants civil rights to improve his lot, to allow him to get a good job and get ahead, to perhaps become one of the economically powerful. Michael suspects that Skinner wants to destroy the whole system and thrust it all into anarchy, that he is one of the 'hooligan element'.

Scene 8 (pp.133–5)

Summary: *Dr Dodds' second speech on poverty; testimony of Brigadier Johnson-Hansbury.*

Explaining again that extreme poverty can make one feel 'inferior, marginal, helpless, dependent', Dr Dodds informs us that these traits can make the subject act impulsively. The extreme poor are 'present-time orientated'; they do not defer gratification or plan for the future (p.133). It is only natural that we associate these characteristics with Skinner. He is clearly impulsive – breaking into display cabinets, drinking the Mayor's liquor, using the phone and so on. But it remains to be seen whether he does this out of the motives put forward by Dr Dodds. Does Skinner behave this way out of feelings of helplessness and inferiority?

In the midst of Dodds' speech, Brigadier Johnson-Hansbury, the commander of the British forces on the day of the killings, gives his testimony to the court of inquiry. He tells of his command, an absolutely monstrous force of personnel and equipment aligned against three unarmed people in a building, and he states uncategorically that the trio 'emerged firing from the Guildhall' (p.134), thus making an arrest impossible.

Earlier, Dr Dodds' first speech was juxtaposed with the speaker at the rally. Similarly, Dodds' second speech is interrupted by the soldier's testimony. It will turn out that Brigadier Johnson-Hansbury told an outright lie in this matter of whether the trio 'emerged firing'.

Q Is Friel suggesting that Dodds too is being untruthful, perhaps without knowing it? Is there something inherently dishonest about trying to lump millions of people throughout the world into one group, claiming that their beliefs, desires and motivations are predictable and quantifiable?

Scene 9 (pp.135–41)

Summary: *In the Parlour: Skinner and Lily play 'dress-up'; they discover the Guildhall has been surrounded; Lily pictures her home.*

Following Dr Dodds' speech, which he finishes by claiming that due to their 'present-orientated living' the poor 'often have a hell of a lot more fun than we have' (p.135), Skinner bursts back into the parlour from the Mayor's dressing room clothed in the full splendour of the Mayor's ceremonial robes. He entices the other two to don robes with him in order to play-act his bestowing upon them 'the freedom of the city'.

Michael takes part reluctantly and only for a moment. Skinner and Lily continue the game, this time pretending they are the Mayor and his wife taking part in a ceremonial parade. Soon they are dancing in the middle of the room to 'The Man Who Broke the Bank'. It's all in fun; Lily takes up Skinner's games without missing a beat, but their levity soon evokes an eruption in Michael:

> MICHAEL: ... I marched three miles today and I attended a peaceful meeting today because every man's entitled to justice and fair play and that's what I'm campaigning for. But this – this – this fooling around, this swaggering about as if you owned the place, this isn't my idea of dignified, peaceful protest. (p.138)

His opinions about Skinner finally show themselves: '... if you ask me, he's more at home with the hooligans, out throwing stones and burning shops!' (p.138). As if to confirm Michael's suspicions, and to show that he does not care, Skinner stubs out his cigar on the leather top of the Mayor's desk. It is the last straw, prompting Michael to decide to leave the parlour. It is only now that Michael and Lily learn what Skinner has obviously known for some time – that the square outside the Guildhall is swarming with soldiers and police.

The freedom of the city

Perhaps Dodds is right: in the face of real danger, Skinner acts irrationally, impulsively. Still, there is something important about the pretend ceremony Skinner puts the others through: 'Don the robes' he says, 'and taste real power' (p.136). He promises to give them 'the freedom of the city'. This phrase needs some explaining.

The freedom of the city is a ceremonial honour bestowed upon important people by the Mayor. It is a welcome and a reward, bestowing the freedom to consider the city your home, to be one of its free citizens. In European cities hundreds of years ago, visitors were not allowed simply to enter a city and settle there; they had to be recognised and approved by the authorities. While the title 'freeman of the city' would be purely ceremonial now, it hearkens back to a time when such status and liberty were hard won and could not be taken for granted.

Skinner recognises the irony of the situation he is in. He and the other marchers have been protesting for the very basic rights that such freedom presumes. They are not at all 'freemen of the city'; they are a subject class being denied their rights. Here in the parlour of the Guildhall, the symbolic home of those who are oppressing them, he cannot resist the delicious irony of going through the mock ceremony (Michael is completely deaf to such irony, of course).

Key point

Under this scenario we could not say that Skinner's levity (his 'having a hell of a lot more fun than we do') is conducted out of the blindness of his 'present-time orientation'. He sees too well; he knows the soldiers are outside and he knows that there will be serious consequences for the trio's having come into this particular room, accidentally or not.

Michael holds fast to his beliefs about dignity and fair treatment. To Skinner he says, 'Now give me one good reason why I can't walk straight out of here and across that Square' (p.140). Skinner's response sums up perfectly the relationship as he sees it between themselves and the forces against which they struggle: 'Because you presumed, boy. Because this is theirs, boy, and your very presence here is a sacrilege' (p.140). Michael quietly acknowledges the truth behind Skinner's words; he does not leave the parlour.

Lily's 'vision' of home

Lily does not take part in the above discourse, but she tries to make peace between the two as best she can. She is not one for political discussions: 'Youse are both away above me' (p.140). As the dispute momentarily grows quiet, Lily, thinking about the chairman and her 'wanes' (children) who will soon be expecting their tea, drifts into a kind of reverie in which she is able to picture with perfect clarity the scene occurring in her over-crowded tenement at that very moment (p.141). Dr Dodds would no doubt call this an 'existential' moment. By that he would mean that Lily's 'present-orientation' is so strong, that she is so tied up in her little world, that she is able to see even the tiniest details of that world. She experiences full appreciation of the moment unencumbered by thoughts of the future. Whether this is really true or not remains to be seen, but it is an extraordinary moment. What Lily may lack in logical thinking, she seems to make up in uncanny perception.

Scene 10 (pp.141–3)

Summary: *The inquiry into whether or not the three were armed continues; Dr Winbourne's forensic report.*

The Judge addresses his courtroom and lets us in on a problem he is having divining the truth. The Priest, who administered the last rites, insists that Skinner, Lily and Michael were unarmed. And the photos by the Photographer show no weapons near the bodies (photographs of dying victims on Bloody Sunday showed a similar situation). But there is 'the sworn testimony of eight soldiers and four policemen' (p.142) insisting that they were fired upon by the trio. As though to decide the issue, the Judge calls in Dr Winbourne, a Scotsman and a forensic expert in the army, to testify on the presence of lead particles on the bodies. The Judge, who earlier admitted he was 'an old army man' himself (p.134), does not see any possible conflict of interest in calling a soldier to give scrutiny to the testimony of other soldiers. Dr Winbourne essentially declares that at least Michael fired a weapon before being fired upon, and that it is possible that Skinner and Lily fired weapons as well. The Judge seems almost to pounce on this erroneous testimony with relief, no doubt calling Lord Widgery to the minds of the original audience (see the notes on Bloody Sunday, pp.4–5 in this Text Guide).

Scene 11 (pp.143–7)

Summary: *Back in the parlour: telephone calls and a 'loudhailer' address.*

Michael notices that more tanks are rolling up outside. Skinner talks Lily into using the phone to call anyone she can think of. It is a comic moment. Lily makes her calls in a 'posh' accent. She enjoys herself. It is even more innocent fun than the dressing up in the mayor's gowns; but Michael still does not like it: 'I want the two of you to know that I object to this carry-on' (p.146). The scene, and Act One, ends with Brigadier Johnson-Hansbury calling in from the Guildhall square and telling the three to come out with their hands up. The final line, delivered by Michael, is the climax of his ongoing disagreement with Skinner. Unable to see why so much force has been mustered against them, he assumes that the soldiers were set off by the violent acts of 'some bloody hooligan! Someone like you, Skinner! For it's bastards like you, bloody vandals, that's keeping us all on our bloody knees!' (p.147).

ACT TWO

Opening (p.148)

Act Two opens with a dramatic echo of Act One: Skinner, Lily and Michael resume the places where their bodies lay when the play began. Now they stand without moving through the song of the Balladeer and the address of the Judge. This play is in part about difference in human perspective. All of the testimony given in the court of inquiry attempts to uncover the truth, to describe what happened that February day when our three characters were killed. The words of the Priest in his church, the songs of the Balladeer, and even the address of Dr Dodds (who, as we've recognised, is not part of the 'action' of the play) – are all testimonies given with the intention of trying to understand Skinner, Lily and Michael or to use them in some way. *We* are getting to understand them in much more depth than they do because the trio's final hours are being performed on stage for us. But to the other characters the three are mute.

Key point

Friel is showing us just how unfair it is that all these other characters are free to create their own stories about the defenceless dead. In the silent presence of Skinner, Lily and Michael, the audience is meant to feel a sense of unfairness that everyone is using these absurd and unnecessary deaths for their own political ends. And they all get the story wrong.

Scene 12 (pp.148–9)

Summary: *The Balladeer's second song and an address by the Judge.*

The Balladeer returns for another song, but this time the tone is sombre and funereal. The defiance and aggression are gone, but this song is still very much about unity and making heroes out of the dead. Martyrs can be much more important to a cause than living fighters.

Following the song is another address to the court by the Judge. His true colours begin to show as he makes a faulty logical supposition. He refers to the trio as the deceased but one can sense that he should really be using the title 'defendants'; it is becoming clear that Skinner, Lily and Michael are the ones on trial, not the soldiers who did the killing. The Judge cannot believe that the trio chose such a symbolic site as the Mayor's parlour purely by accident. Then he confirms his belief by citing the minor vandalism that occurred to the room and its contents.

The conclusion is faulty because it works backwards: the fact that the three did some damage must mean that they had intended to go there all along: 'No other conclusion is consistent with the facts' (p.149). Yet there is no evidence for this at all. He never considers that they might have come upon the place accidentally and only committed the vandalism after they realised *where* they were. In an actual court of justice, such a conclusion could not go unchallenged. But this is a court of inquiry, one with much lower standards of proof; the Judge is responsible only for coming up with 'an objective view of the events'. He may believe he is being objective, but it is becoming apparent that the tribunal is working towards a completely subjective interpretation of the day's events.

Key point

Note how Friel reinforces this conclusion by juxtaposing the song of the Balladeer and the address of the Judge. On the face of it, no two things could be more opposite. The song is emotional, biased, and inflammatory. The address is precise, rational, unemotional and ostensibly objective. But we are beginning to recognise that the Judge's words are just as biased as the Balladeer's, and they are just as political.

Scene 13 (pp.149–50)

Summary: *Skinner, Lily and Michael speak of their deaths.*

As though responding to the injustice of being unable to tell their stories while every one around them creates false versions of their lives, the trio tells us about the very moments of their deaths.

Michael describes his absolute surprise at the moment of death (pp.149–50). That the soldiers might shoot had never entered as a possibility into his understanding of the situation. Though he knew there were violent people on both sides of the conflict, he also believed fervently that the other side would deal fairly with them if they were peaceful and maintained their dignity: 'I knew they weren't going to shoot. Shooting belonged to a different order of things' (p.149). He dies believing that a terrible mistake has been made, 'in disbelief, in astonishment, in shock' (p.150). His final statement, 'It was a foolish way for a man to die' (p.150), hints that he has perhaps come to realise the mistakes of his philosophy in dealing with the other side, but this is not necessarily so. Michael is an idealist; it is no surprise that he is murdered believing a mistake has been made. He may have been naive, but this does not mean there is anything wrong with his idealism.

Lily feels 'a tidal wave of regret', not for her death or for her family but because 'life had somehow eluded [her]' (p.150). What she means by this is that she had never stopped to really look at her life, to really consider it all the time she was so busy living it. Dr Dodds' words about present-orientated living might ring in our ears as might a quote attributed to Socrates: 'The unexamined life is not worth living'. There is a paradox at work here. Lily is the one who seems to have almost absolute clarity of vision when it comes to seeing what her neighbours must be doing in their tenement. She is brimming with stories about the chairman, her 'wanes', her relations, even the grocer. In all this time, apparently, she was seeing without digesting what she saw, without taking it in and understanding. She believes her life to have been without meaning. This is the source of her regret: 'In a way I died of grief'.

Skinner was much less surprised by the killings than Michael or Lily: 'A short time after I realised we were in the Mayor's parlour I knew that a price would be exacted … I began to suspect what that price would be because they leave nothing to chance and because the poor are always overcharged' (p.150). As Michael moves a little closer to Skinner's way of seeing things in death, Skinner moves towards Michael's. He sees just how serious the other side is about the protesters and how relatively lightly he has been taking them. He sounds a bit like Michael when he says 'to match their seriousness would demand a total dedication, a solemnity as formal as theirs'. But of course Skinner does not possess such solemnity. He dies making a joke to himself, in 'defensive flippancy'.

Q These revelations from beyond death are a Brechtian attempt to break the spell of realism on the audience. What other purposes do they serve? Why do the three characters lose their accents and their idiosyncratic ways of speaking?

Scene 14 (pp.150–1)

Summary: *The Judge speaks to his courtroom.*

He is still trying to resolve the issue of whether the trio fired weapons upon the soldiers before being killed. He will call a pathologist to testify the next day.

Scene 15 (pp.151–5)

Summary: *In the parlour: Lily and Skinner discuss why they march.*

Skinner makes a telling remark on the plight of the poor: 'If I'm sick, the entire wisdom of the health authority is at my service. And should I die, the welfare people would bury me in style. It's only when I'm alive and well that I'm a problem' (p.152). In his ironic way, Skinner raises a depressing truth. The poor are inconvenient to the dominant culture.

We see more of Skinner's 'defensive flippancy' when Lily makes the kind offer of 'a bite to eat most days of the week' (p.152) and with thirteen mouths to feed. Skinner, after a pause, goes into another round of play, taking the ceremonial sword and pretending to duel with it. A person like Skinner, who has been on his own from the age of eleven, bristles not only at those he mistrusts or dislikes; he is likely to be defensive against even those who offer him comfort and goodwill. It is part of the survival instinct of one for whom survival is a constant challenge. Lily's question to him concerning his mock duel: 'Who are you fighting?' (p.153) is meaningful on more than one level.

In a more serious vein, Skinner asks Lily: 'Has it anything at all to do with us?' (p.153). By 'us' he means the poor. He takes Michael's ideas about the protests ('doctors, plumbers, teachers, accountants, all shoulder to shoulder') to task. Does it really have anything to do with them? Will the poor ever get a fair deal? If civil rights do come will they make any difference? He wants to know why Lily marches, and when she offers nothing but vague echoes of the rhetoric she would have heard at rallies, he offers his own suggestion:

> SKINNER: ... Because for the first time in your life you grumbled and someone else grumbled and someone else, and you heard each other, and became aware that there were hundreds, thousands, millions of us all over the world, and in a vague groping way you were outraged ... It's about us – the poor – the majority – stirring in our sleep. (p.154)

Key point

Skinner's explanation is exactly consistent with Dr Dodds' first speech about the objectivity that can compel the poor to become politically active. Once they expand their awareness and realise that they belong to a group of millions around the world who are disenfranchised, they gain some chance of gaining a political voice.

Lily's response is noncommittal: 'I suppose you're right'. These aren't Lily's reasons, though clearly they are Skinner's. We can infer that Skinner must have indeed been on the march; he is not one of the hooligans, but he marches for a reason different from Michael's. He marches for the poor like himself who have little voice in this world and who 'are always overcharged'.

Lily tells Skinner why she really marches. Her son Declan has Down's syndrome. She uses the term 'mongol' which was common at the time – it came from a culturally insensitive and inept observation that children born with this condition looked like people from Mongolia. She observes that marching will certainly make no difference to Declan; it's important to realise that she is not marching for better treatment or care or medicines for her son. She says it's a stupid thing to do. But she marches anyway, for Declan, every Saturday.

Scene 16 (pp.155–6)

Summary: *The Priest's second speech – on the subject of the march and the deaths of Skinner, Lily and Michael.*

In another address to his congregation the Priest speaks about some of the desires (gainful employment, decent housing, effective voting) that might have motivated the protest march and demonstration that led to the deaths of Skinner, Lily and Michael. The address turns to railing against the 'revolutionaries' (to the Priest the term is synonymous with Communists) who he worries have taken over the movement. It should be remembered that there is no greater enemy to the Catholic Church than Communism (certainly not the Protestant authority ruling Northern Ireland) because Communism embraces the doctrine of atheism.

> PRIEST: ... I don't suggest for one minute that the three people who died yesterday were part of this conspiracy, were even aware that they were victims of this conspiracy. But victims they were ... let me quote to you from that most revolutionary of doctrines – the sermon on the mount: 'Blessed are the meek for they shall possess the land.' (p.156)

It is important here to remember the context: this is supposed to be a time of mourning for the three victims, and the Priest is turning it into a political opportunity. In this he has sunk himself to the level of the Balladeer and the Judge. It shows, again, that there is no consensus among the oppressed; they fight amongst themselves as violently, perhaps more violently, than they do against the oppressors. The fight against Communism is so important to the Priest that it is worth defacing the memory of the dead. Even though he claims not to suggest that Skinner, Lily and Michael *were* Communists, his bringing up the subject does just that; and it is worth dragooning some of the most poignant words from Christ's Sermon on the Mount into a purely political struggle. Surely this is sacrilegious. His reminder that the meek shall inherit the earth has about it the noble air of nonviolent protest, but the Priest uses it as a stick against the Communists and not as an incentive to follow the doctrines of Ghandi (whom Michael mentioned earlier) or Martin Luther King.

Q What do you think Friel is saying about the role of the Catholic clergy in 'the Troubles' in Northern Ireland?

Scene 17 (pp.156–61)

Summary: *The penultimate scene in the Mayor's parlour: Skinner reads the minutes; Michael talks about his reasons for marching.*

Michael returns from the dressing room to get everyone ready to surrender to the soldiers. Skinner immediately goes back into flippant mode, a little more aggressively even than before. Michael wants to maintain control – 'Will you listen to me!' (p.158) he demands, as though he were organising their walk out of the parlour as a protest march. Skinner plays one last game, reading the minutes of a council meeting. There is a sense that Skinner is delaying the moment of leaving, yet there is something meaningful in what he reads. It is the ordinary business of a city council – subscriptions to the RSPCA, a request from the District Floral Society, tenders for painting public buildings, etc. Pretty dull stuff, but consider that this, in effect, is what our three characters will *die* for. Everyone sees their accidental occupation of the Mayor's office as a political act – the Judge speaks of their deliberately 'defacing' and 'defiling' this symbolic office (p.149). Surely Friel wants us to consider the kind of people who are ready to kill and condemn to protect the sanctity of an office whose business is Rugby club petitions and Amateur Opera Society buffet suppers.

There is another layer of irony in how far removed from Skinner's vagabond existence and Lily's tenement world these very middle class items are. Skinner teases Michael:

> SKINNER: ... As one of the city's nine thousand unemployed isn't it in your interest that your idleness is pursued in an environment as pleasant as possible with pets and flowers and music and gaily painted buildings? (p.160)

Symbolism

There is some significant symbolism evident in this office. As petty as these items on the mayoral agenda are, they stand for all the things being denied to our three characters, to the 'fourteen per cent', the unemployed living in poverty – the subject class.

This scene gives Michael a chance to crystallise his desires for us. What he wants is very simple: 'a decent job, a decent place to live, a decent town to bring up our children in ... And we want fair play, too, so that ... we have the same chances and the same opportunities as the next fella' (pp.160–1). It would be very difficult to argue with these demands. But there is no reason that we need to take sides, Skinner against Michael or vice versa. There is no 'right' opinion amongst the three protesters. Michael may be a bit naive in Skinner's eyes, but he wants basic rights; he is correct when he says, 'we'll get it, because it's something every man's entitled to' (p.161). Friel *does* want us to see that they are different, and that no political movement is homogeneous.

Scene 18 (pp.161–2)

Summary: *Testimony: Professor Cuppley presents his report on the post-mortems.*

Professor Cuppley's testimony about the post-mortem conducted on the three gives brutal details of the work done by the SLR rifles of the soldiers. Dramatically, this scene is a brief pause before the climax we are rapidly approaching. We know that Skinner, Lily and Michael are only minutes away from walking out to their deaths. It is a pause, but the testimony also heightens the tension; its graphic nature reinforces the terrible human price the three characters pay for their innocent mistake.

Q The Judge had implied in Scene 14 that Professor Cuppley's evidence would throw needed light on the question of whether the three were armed when they left the Guildhall. Does it?

Scene 19 (p.163)

Summary: *Dr Dodds' final speech – the gulf between the rich and the poor.*

Almost like a Greek chorus summing up the meaning of the events we've been witnessing, Dr Dodds wraps up his imaginary conference speech with rather dire warnings about the growing gap between rich and poor throughout the world and about the future for this subculture. Even if we conclude that Dr Dodds' theories have limited applicability to our three characters, his final words about people in their position bear thinking about as we contemplate the fate about to meet them:

> DODDS: ... They become more and more estranged from the dominant society. Their position becomes more and more insecure. They have, in fact, no future. They have only today. And if they fail to cope with today, the only certainty they have is death. (p.163)

Scene 20 (pp.163–6)

Summary: *Final scene in the Mayor's parlour: signing the guestbook and a final discussion between Michael and Skinner before meeting their deaths.*

Skinner's sense of estrangement can also be seen in his virtual last act. Having driven the ceremonial sword into the staid portrait of Sir Joshua, he demands that Michael leave it alone, saying, 'Allow me my gesture' (p.163). The gesture is not necessarily violent, nor does it necessarily mean that Skinner really is one of the 'revolutionaries' that Michael or the Priest decries (though he may be – we do not know the answer). But it certainly shows us that Skinner feels he is fighting not just the British soldiers, but the whole weight of history. He does not just want 'the same opportunities as the next fella' (p.161); he wants to dismantle completely what to him is a master/slave relationship. Only when it is gone can true civil rights begin.

Key point

With the exception of the sword in the portrait and the signing of the visitors' book (and the possible exception of the cigar burn on the desk), the three return the parlour to the condition it was before they entered it. Remember that the Judge takes it upon himself to conclude – by the evidence of the way the rooms and records were 'defaced' and 'despoiled' – that Skinner, Lily and Michael had planned all along to occupy the Guildhall.

The signing of the Distinguished Visitors' Book is truly the last act. Lily writes her name as grandly as she can and next to it puts 'looking forward to a return visit'. The irony here does not require comment – she will be dead in a few minutes, but it is matched by the comment Skinner attaches to his name: 'Freeman of the city' (p.165). When Lily, not understanding the term, says, 'Sure that means nothing', Skinner responds 'I suppose you're right, Lily' (p.165). Again, though he is free to knock about as he will, venturing as far as England and Scotland, Skinner will never be a 'freeman' in the city of his birth. And perhaps people like him and Lily and Michael can never really be free anywhere.

The last discussion Michael and Skinner have shows their continued difference in the perception of the 'enemy'. Now Michael mocks Skinner: 'You really think they'd shoot you! You really do!' (p.166). Skinner knows full well that they may. Michael believes to the end that his enemies are as reasonable as he. He fails to understand what Skinner knows instinctively: to the soldiers and those whose bidding they do, he, Lily and Michael simply do not register as 'reasonable', thinking human beings. They are 'terrorists', the enemy, the refuse of Bogside.

Lily's last act is to welcome the two young men to her meagre home anytime they choose to come. Michael's is to take control of the situation and offer his cooperation to the enemy he is sure will act reasonably and judiciously. Skinner's, after an uncharacteristic expression of tenderness, a kiss on Lily's forehead, is to exit in flippancy, singing 'The Man Who Broke the Bank'. They meet their ends within character.

Epilogue (pp.167–9)

Summary: *The funeral – Liam O'Kelly's report and the Judge's findings.*

Liam O'Kelly reports on the funeral for his Dublin television station. There is considerable irony on this sombre occasion. The list of dignitaries in attendance includes the Cardinal Primate, the full houses of government in the Irish Republic, even the Irish Taoiseach (Prime Minister). They are inside the church while the residents of Bogside wait outside in the rain.

This list of 'distinguished visitors' reminds us of the Distinguished Visitors' Book that the Judge determines Skinner and Lily to have defiled. If the 'distinguished' had afforded the three, and those like them, even a portion of the attention they give now, they would surely not have died. But perhaps of more importance is the irony that even in death, the trio continues to be watched and commented upon, their motives dissected and discussed.

We can feel safe in assuming that they continue to be utterly misunderstood by those who use them for political gain. O'Kelly, with the pomposity that only a news reporter can attain, rhapsodises on how 'dignified' the occasion is. Not mentioned is how the actions of the British soldiers, and after them the British inquiry, strip the three of any dignity at all.

The Judge's conclusions

The Judge's final address underscores these bitter ironies. Not surprisingly he finds everyone except those who pulled the trigger – the marchers, the demonstrators, the victims themselves – responsible for the deaths of Skinner, Lily and Michael (see 'Themes, Ideas & Values' for a fuller discussion of the Judge's findings). During the Judge's speech, Skinner, Lily and Michael stand in their original places and stare out mutely at the audience. Again we are left with the feeling that while the sanctioned representative of their oppressors (the Judge) is allowed to misrepresent them, they are robbed of their voices. The Judge talks of passing on his findings to the appropriate authorities, but the Skinners and Lilys and

Michaels of the world have no higher authority to take their case to, no place to get a fair hearing.

Gunfire

Friel ends the play with something we might not have noticed was missing before, the sound of gunfire. In the scene where the three finally march out of the Guildhall, they do so to the sound of organ music played at their funeral. The sound of automatic fire that kills them is supplied here while the trio continues to stare at the audience. The effect is powerful – a very dramatic way to end a play that so shockingly began with three corpses lying across the apron of the stage.

The Judge's conclusion

The gunfire also signifies something else. The Judge's conclusion, which is essentially a verdict passed upon three people who were never supposed to be on trial, amounts to the final act in the murder of the three. The soldiers only pulled the trigger. It is the Judge (and what he represents) who tries hardest to snuff out the life of these and any others who would shift the balance of power away from the dominant order. He does so by manipulating one of the most powerful apparatuses of the dominators, the legal system.

Key point

The Judge is changing the story, commandeering it, to suit his purposes. The lamentable tale of three innocents caught in the crossfire becomes the 'official' case of three 'terrorists' who took over a government building and tried to shoot their way out. He is killing them all over again.

CHARACTERS & RELATIONSHIPS

A chorus of commentators: Dr Dodds, the Balladeer, the Priest, Liam O'Kelly

There are two main groups of characters in *The Freedom of the City*: Skinner, Lily and Michael, and all those who comment on them. While everyone besides the three main characters belongs in this latter group, the more important ones are those I have selected (the Judge is discussed later). They represent, in order:

- the international, liberal intelligentsia – Dr Dodds
- the working class, grassroots Irish unity movement – the Balladeer
- the Catholic Church – the Priest
- the international media – Liam O'Kelly.

A kind of modern Greek chorus

Considered together, they are quite a diverse group but can be seen as a kind of modern Greek chorus. In ancient Greek plays a group of performers called 'the chorus' would comment on the actions of the play without actually being a part of it. They were representatives of the playwright who could explain or interpret scenes.

Key point

The 'chorus of commentators' in *The Freedom of the City* are representatives of the most powerful forces at play in the 'intellectual' debate about civil rights in Northern Ireland. Like a chorus, their only source of power is in their opinions.

Dr Dodds

Key quotes

'People with a culture of poverty are provincial and locally orientated and have very little sense of history.' (p.111)

'But the very moment they acquire an objective view of their condition ... they have broken out of their subculture, even though they may still be desperately poor.' (p.111)

'And of course the economic environment conditions the psychological and social man so that he constantly feels inferior, marginal, helpless, dependent ... he is present-time orientated and seldom defers gratification ...' (p.133)

'... they often have a hell of a lot more fun than we have.' (p.135)

'They have only today. And if they fail to cope with today, the only certainty they have is death.' (p.163)

Dr Dodds is the only one of this group whose physical existence is totally unrelated to the setting or time frame of the play. For this reason it is easy to think of him as being purely a representative of the opinions of the playwright, and further, to think of these opinions as infallible. But we should be careful. If Dodds were *just* Friel's chorus, he may not have been given a specific identity (Greek choruses are not given individual identities). He is not just a disembodied voice, but an individual, subject to the misapprehensions and errors that anyone might make.

Why an American?

There is probably a very simple reason for Dodds' American nationality. It allows him presumptive political neutrality not possible in an Irishman or an Englishman. His position as a scientist also presumes neutrality; scientists are supposed to be interested in the truth without bias. Yet is he unbiased? Many conservatives would see his explanations of the plight of the poor as quite radical.

Dodds seems to take on the role of the chorus in that the three characters in the parlour seem to respond to comments he makes. He speaks of the 'fun' that present-time orientation can grant to the poor, and within moments Skinner is dressing up as the Mayor (Scene 9). But the closer we look at these situations, the more it is revealed that Dr Dodds' theories are applicable only to a certain point. He may be correct about some of Lily's traits, but he is totally wrong about her reasons for joining the protest march, for instance. He focuses the attention of the audience on very interesting and relevant issues concerning the politics of this play, but his position of authority is problematic. Surely the play is trying to show us that there is no homogeneity, no sameness, to what Dodds calls the 'subculture' of extreme poverty. That subculture is composed of individuals with their own behaviours.

The Balladeer

Key quotes

'Three cheers and then three cheers again for Ireland one and free,
For civil rights and unity, Tone, Pearce and Connolly.' (p.118)

'We'll not forget that sunny evening, nor the names of those bold three
Who gave their lives for their ideal – Mother Ireland, one and free.' (p.148)

As a person, the Balladeer is no more than the cultural stereotype of the drunken Irishman. His importance comes from his function. He resembles the Greek chorus in being only a mouthpiece, without any authentic individual characteristics. An agent for reunification, he is the personification of that aspect of any political movement that makes heroes and legends out of the common men and women who give their lives to the cause. The Balladeer just happens to employ a particularly 'Irish' version of such mythmaking: the drinking song. In a larger context, the Balladeer represents some of the emotional intensity without which the oppressed in Bogside – or anywhere else in the world – could never rouse themselves to face the vast forces lined up against them. This is how he represents a 'way of thinking' that is crucial to understanding this play.

The Priest

Key quotes

'They sacrificed their lives so that you and I and thousands like us might be rid of that iniquitous yoke and might inherit a decent way of life.' (p.125)

'Who are they, these evil people? I will speak and I will speak plainly ... they have one purpose and one purpose only – to deliver this Christian country into the dark dungeons of Godless communism.' (p.156)

'I don't suggest for one minute that the three people who died yesterday were part of this conspiracy ... But victims they were.' (p.156)

The Priest (Father Brosnan) is first seen administering to the souls of the deceased with the last rites. This is one of his most important offices. It is only when the Priest makes political judgements from his pulpit that he takes on the role of commentator. He represents in part the complicated role that the Catholic Church has played in all Irish political movements. He is clearly a supporter of the cause of civil rights, but most emphatically not of its Communist element. Friel no doubt wants us to see that terrible complications can set in when spiritual leaders, with their enormous persuasive power, begin to play politics.

Liam O'Kelly

Key quotes

'... unconfirmed reports are coming in that a group of about fifty armed gunmen have taken possession of the Guildhall ...' (p.117)

'And if one were to search for a word that would best describe the atmosphere here today, the tenor of the proceedings, the attitude of the ordinary people, I think the word would be dignified.' (p.168)

O'Kelly is a television reporter for *Telefis Eireann* (Irish Television) in Dublin. Unlike the other members of our 'chorus of commentators', O'Kelly does not offer opinions; he simply reports the 'facts' as he gathers them. It is when he reports what is not confirmed that he is dangerous. The influence of the media is enormous; they are, in a sense, 'the eyes of the world'. Coming from the Irish Republic, he would naturally be viewed with hostility by the British soldiers. There is thus some irony in the fact that O'Kelly's inflammatory reporting plays its part in getting Skinner, Lily and Michael killed.

These commentators direct the audience's ideas in their various ways. Think of the ways they represent Skinner, Lily and Michael. To Dodds they are specimens of a subculture whose actions and beliefs can be observed, analysed and predicted. To the Balladeer they are legendary heroes, sacrificing themselves to a cause none of them even mentions. To the Priest they are Christian martyrs and pawns in the fight against Communism. To Liam O'Kelly they are 'fifty armed gunmen'. We, who know far more than they about the three characters, can see how wrong each of these conclusions is.

Key point

We might conclude that together they really form a parody of a Greek chorus; they speak as though blessed with divine authority, but no one gets the story right.

The Judge and his tribunal of inquiry – the voice of judgement

Key quotes

'Our only function is to form an objective view of the events ...' (p.109)

'... their action was a carefully contrived act of defiance against, and an incitement to others to defy, the legitimate forces of law and order. No other conclusion is consistent with the facts.' (p.149)

'There would have been no deaths in Londonderry on February 10 had the ban on the march and the meeting been respected ...' (p.168)

'There is no reason to suppose that the soldiers would have opened fire if they had not been fired on first.' (p.168)

The Judge, an elderly Englishman, is not given a name; he is much more important as a function than as an individual. The Judge is meant to represent objectivity and unbiased inquiry, but we have reason to doubt his impartiality in this matter, pitting Irish citizens against British soldiers. Starting off as an impartial investigator, he ends up as a symbol of institutionalised prejudice (in both capacities his namelessness is perfectly appropriate; see 'Themes, Ideas & Values'). But it should be clear throughout the play that the Judge's final assessment is a foregone conclusion.

Q Does the Judge *deliberately* ignore the testimony to reach his conclusions? Or is it just that for him British soldiers who knowingly shoot unarmed civilians more than thirty times with automatic weapons simply 'belong to a different order of things' (to borrow Michael's phrase)?

Key point

The most important aspect of this character is his transformation from symbol of objectivity to political mouthpiece. This transformation runs parallel to the Judge's subtly shifting the intention of his inquiry from an ostensibly objective investigation into a trial (in all but name) of Skinner, Lily and Michael. As noted earlier, the Judge becomes their judge; and in a symbolic way he also becomes their executioner.

Michael Hegarty

Key quotes

'I'm going to the tech. four nights a week – you know – to improve myself.' (p.122)

'I've been on every civil rights march from the very beginning – right from October 5th.' (p.127)

'The ultimate objectives we're all striving for is more important than the personalities or the politics of the individuals concerned.' (p.127)

'And that's what we must show them – that we're responsible and respectable; and they'll come to respect what we're campaigning for.' (pp.128–9)

'... some bloody hooligan! Someone like you, Skinner! For it's bastards like you, bloody vandals, that's keeping us all on our bloody knees!' (p.147)

Key quotes

'But there was no question of their shooting. I knew they weren't going to shoot. Shooting belonged to a totally different order of things.' (p.149)

'And we want fair play, too, so that no matter what our religion is, no matter what our politics is, we have the same chances and the same opportunities as the next fella.' (p.161)

Michael Hegarty is the most straightforward of the three main protagonists. He is an earnest young man with strong beliefs about the cause of civil rights. He has been on all the marches since the first and worries that they are becoming less dignified. He loathes what he calls the 'hooligan element' that is more interested in destruction and violence than in civil rights. He believes in the principles of civil disobedience, as espoused by Ghandi, that rights can best be gained through nonviolent protest. He is certain that if the protesters show themselves as rational, peaceful and dignified they will eventually win the respect of their overlords and thus gain the rights they seek. These beliefs seem firm in the face of setbacks that could easily give them a bit of a shake. Michael has been unemployed for some time; every job he holds seems to vanish as his employers are driven out of business. He believes in the future; while waiting for work, he takes night classes at the local tech in subjects chosen to give him the best opportunity for making it in the world.

Michael's convictions and his optimism are admirable, yet he does not understand the forces he is contending with. The results of the inquiry show us that no measure of dignity and reason is going to prompt the British to treat Michael and his fellows as anything but terrorists. He dies in utter disbelief that soldiers would fire on *him*. There is also a telling rigidity about Michael. He condemns any members of the movement who do not share his particular convictions; to him they are hooligans and revolutionaries. When this exclusiveness is compounded with his naivity, Michael is at his most flawed. At the end of Act One he screams at Skinner: 'it's bastards like you, bloody vandals, that's keeping us all on our bloody knees!' It is of course not people like Skinner who are keeping them on their knees, it is their oppressors who are doing it, the government of Northern Ireland and its British supporters. Like the Priest, Michael is too subject to the internecine rhetoric that he forgets who the real enemy is.

Lily – Elizabeth M Doherty

Key quotes

'Lookat, young fella: since it was the British troops driv me off my own streets and deprived me of my sight and vision for a good quarter of an hour, the least the corporation can do is placate me with one wee drink.' (p.121)

'Me? I could never do nothing right at school except carry round the roll books. And when the inspector would come they used to lock me in the cloakroom with the Mad Mulligans.' (p.122)

'Mother of God, if the wanes could see me now!' (p.136)

'And down the passage aul Andy Boyle's lying in bed because he has no coat. And I'm here in the Mayor's parlour, dressed up like the Duchess of Kent and drinking port wine. I'll tell you something, Skinner: it's a very unfair world.' (p.141)

'... I thought I glimpsed a tiny truth: that life had eluded me because never once in my forty-three years had an experience, an event, even a small unimportant happening been isolated, and assessed, and articulated.' (p.150)

'You and him ... and everybody else marching and protesting about sensible things like politics and stuff and me in the middle of you all, marching for Declan. Isn't that the stupidest thing you ever heard?' (p.155)

Elizabeth Doherty is a more complicated character than she might at first seem. On the surface she is quite a stereotype: the ignorant Irish Catholic woman lorded over by a lazy and brutal husband for whom she only apologises. She has squeezed out children until there are evidently none left. She works her fingers to the bone to feed her enormous family without complaining, without seeming even to wonder about something different. But these stereotyped qualities really describe her circumstances only. And while her gossipy discourse and her colourful expressions also seem fairly stereotyped, Lily reveals her own identity despite them.

Lily, of our three main characters, and indeed among all the characters in the play, is the only one who does not hesitate in revealing herself. Yes, her actions bespeak kind-heartedness, and her instinct is to mother. But it is in her speech that she really gives of herself. Skinner and Michael (as well as the audience) learn so much about her in so little time because she holds nothing back. There is a generosity of spirit that has nothing to do with kind words or gifts, but only with letting strangers 'in' and making them no longer strangers.

Michael is rather reticent with Lily. The two characters do not 'connect' in the way that Lily and Skinner do. After a rocky start – she calls Skinner a 'brat' after one of his more cheeky comments (p.132) – a definite tenderness springs up between Lily and Skinner. It would be easy to put this down to Lily's mothering quality and Skinner's unconscious need for a surrogate mother, but that is not the extent of their mutual regard. Lily is a lot of fun. She takes up Skinner's games with spirit and a surprising liveliness of mind. She brings none of Skinner's cynicism (or his politics) to these games, yet he identifies with her sense of fun and adventure anyway. She drinks her 'port wine' and enjoys the moment. This all indicates an almost superhuman resiliency in the face of a life that would destroy many.

Dramatically, she is something like an umpire in the running battle between Skinner and Michael over the way the civil rights cause should proceed. Even before their differences begin to show themselves, Lily positions herself between the two of them. She tries to make peace when they are sparring verbally.

Lily fits Dr Dodds' descriptions of the subculture of poverty better than either Skinner or Michael, yet she also defies those descriptions. She is certainly 'present-time orientated', and Dodds' remarks about the poor really knowing only their own very limited world are applicable to her. But her knowledge of that world transcends Dodds' disparaging words about it in its artistic intensity; moreover, this intensity indicates a deep concern. Lily understands her world because she shares in its problems, in a word, because she cares. And so she marches – not because she has come to an objective understanding of the plight of the poor around the world (as Dodds would have it); she marches for what she calls a 'stupid' reason, because her son Declan has Down's syndrome. It is totally futile, but she marches anyway, every Saturday (she could be at home with her feet up after her difficult week). It may be in their most futile acts that people truly reveal themselves. Some engage in pointless violence or destruction (the hooligan element) and allow the great emptiness of their character to show. Others take on futile acts of kindness and reveal their richness.

Lily is the most 'human' of the three characters. Through her more than the others, Friel is putting a face and a history to the numbers out in the streets attempting to change things. And more than either Skinner or Michael, Lily's character makes this more than a merely 'political' play. She generates old-fashioned Aristotelian pity in the audience; we identify with her in ways that we cannot with the other two. None of them deserve to die, obviously, and the tragic quality of the violent deaths of two men in their early twenties is enormous. But the fate of Lily with her eleven children in her two-room tenement and the husband who calls her 'a bone stupid bitch' (p.155) is heartbreaking, even *before* the violent death that might seem like the brutal punch line to some ghastly joke.

Skinner – Adrian Casimir Fitzgerald

Key quotes

'Mayor's robes, alderman's robes, councillor's robes. Put them on and I'll give you both the freedom of the city.' (p.135)

'Because you presumed, boy. Because this is theirs, boy, and your very presence here is a sacrilege.' (p.140)

'... as we stood on the Guildhall steps, two thoughts raced through my mind: how seriously they took us and how unpardonably casual we were about them ... And my last thought was: if you're going to decide to take them on, Adrian Casimir, you've got to mend your ways. So I died, as I lived, in defensive flippancy.' (p.150)

Key quotes

'If I'm sick, the entire wisdom of the health authority is at my service. And should I die, the welfare people would bury me in style. It's only when I'm alive and well that I'm a problem.' (p.152)

'It has nothing to do with doctors and accountants and teachers and dignity and boy scout honour. It's about us – the poor – the majority – stirring in our sleep.' (p.154)

Skinner is quite a complex character. Though he never had much schooling, he is intelligent. Friel calls his a 'quick volatile mind' in the introductory directions (p.103). He is not merely a practical joker. Skinner's flippant remarks come from a serious and angry mind. They are meant to bite. He would seem to fit in neatly with Dr Dodds' comments that the poor are able to have a 'hell of a lot more fun than we have' (p.135); but in Skinner fun can seem beside the point. In his brief speech about the moment of his death, he calls his flippancy 'defensive'. It serves the purpose of keeping the world at arm's length, the only way that he can cope with his circumstances. Instead of giving way to violence or abject depression about the unfairness in his life or in the world at large, Skinner jokes. He was orphaned as a baby and brought up by an aunt who died when he was eleven. He has lived on his wits since then.

Despite his threadbare appearance – he is wearing canvas shoes without socks and only a shirt with no jacket or undershirt in the middle of winter – Skinner has the air of possibility and freedom. The latter is a paramount theme with Skinner. He obviously believes he is being denied full freedom, as evidenced by his constant reference to 'the freedom of the city'. It is through Skinner that one of Friel's most important themes is raised: who is free? What does freedom really mean? Skinner is not free because he belongs to a subject class. Again, his views on the plight of his class seem to fit in perfectly with what Dr Dodds describes in the poor as 'an objective view of their condition'. To Skinner the struggle is based on class; it is about the poor, 'stirring in [their] sleep'. He wants nothing to do with Michael's idyll of doctors and accountants marching together with the poor for civil rights. Skinner's outlook is radical, perhaps even revolutionary. But we cannot say with confidence that Skinner is one of the 'hooligans'.

Having dealt all his life with the authorities, Skinner knows how naive is Michael's approach to the British. Of the three, Skinner is the first to realise that they are surrounded, and he is the only one to realise the extent of the danger. While Michael is preparing to give his name and address if questioned, Skinner is seriously wondering if they will be murdered.

Skinner has a very human side beyond the flippancy. A certain tenderness springs up between him and Lily. He is obviously touched by her plight, just as she is by his. He sees that her reason for marching is not stupid. Skinner seems to want to promote himself as being self-serving (Michael is essentially accusing him of this when he calls him a hooligan – the hooligans are willing to sacrifice the good of the cause for the sake of their own enjoyment or rage). But Skinner's relationship with Lily betrays a very human empathy (think how much of his energies are spent on making sure she has a good time on her afternoon in the parlour; he looks after her more than she does him). He is only partly successful in masking it with flippancy. Like Lily, Skinner cares. It shows him to be more than just a mouthpiece for a political position.

Other minor characters

It is important to note that other minor characters are important for the functions they perform and for the ways in which they represent various authorities.

The Policeman gives information about the 'deceased' in a detached, formulaic way using the language of 'facts' to set the scene at the tribunal of inquiry. While he repeats that he wasn't the first at the scene and that he saw no weapons, this information is overlooked later.

The Soldiers appear very early (p.108) to drag the bodies away. They are fully armed and fearful. They reappear later (p.117) when they learn that someone is inside the Guildhall and they send for reinforcements.

The Army Press Officer (p.126) reads a press release that gives inflammatory information – that forty people have taken possession of the Guildhall, two soldiers have been injured but no civilians. Press questions reveal the falseness of his answers – that the whole first floor is occupied and the occupiers have access to arms. He refuses to answer questions about the number of men at his disposal and why the Guildhall wasn't guarded.

Brigadier Johnson-Hansbury, in charge of security on that day, reveals the enormous number of men and the range of equipment at his disposal (p.133). The Judge, 'an old army man', suggests that the Brigadier had 'a rather formidable array to line up against three terrorists' (p.134) – note the word 'terrorists' here. The Brigadier is required to give critical 'evidence' as to why the three were shot rather than being arrested. He claims that because they emerged from the Guildhall firing, it was impossible to arrest them. Even though he thought they were at the front of a larger group about to emerge, he would not have changed his tactics if he had known that there were only three people involved.

Dr Winbourne of the Army Forensic Department gives evidence allegedly based on scientific information that could explain the presence of lead particles on each of the deceased (pp.142–3). Even though he claims that Hegarty could have been 'contaminated while ... being carried away by the soldiers who shot them' (p.143), he admits, with some prompting from the Judge, that he is personally convinced that Hegarty did fire a gun. This is heard in court despite his statement that he 'is a scientist' and does not 'know what constitutes conclusive evidence' (p.142).

Q Look carefully at each person's information. Do they just give the 'facts'?

Q Are all of these authorities prejudiced against the trio? How do the Judge's responses to these individuals' evidence show that he is not impartial?

THEMES, IDEAS & VALUES

The Freedom of the City is a political play. The specific issues it addresses concerning the issues of civil rights and repression in Northern Ireland in the early 1970s are powerful, but the play's importance is not limited to that. If it were, you would not be reading it so many years later in a country so far away. Before turning to the specifics, we'll look at some of the general themes of the play.

Justice and prejudice

Let's return to the play's opening, with its three bodies lying on stage and the court of inquiry beginning its investigation. These elements can easily put us in mind of a murder mystery. But this is a false scent – a red herring. This play has none of the hallmarks of that genre. To begin with, there is never any doubt about who commits the killings. The further the Judge goes with his investigation, the further he gets from the truth. His concluding address is exactly the opposite of the 'unveiling' typical to the denouement of a murder mystery – it covers the truth with a false version designed to maintain the status quo.

Still, this model is helpful in seeing the importance of Friel's theme. If murder mysteries are about the pursuit of justice in the face of misleading clues or false appearances, *The Freedom of the City* is about dressing up prejudice and calling it justice. The truth is either abandoned utterly or forced to conform to a paradigm (model) that has been determined before any facts are heard. This, Friel tells us, is the nature of power politics. In order to maintain hegemony (predominance, dominant influence), the ruling elite cannot allow themselves to be shown to be in the wrong, even if doing so requires twisting facts or offending against the rules of logic. The Judge proves this in his suppositions about Skinner, Lily and Michael's motives in entering the Mayor's parlour and in his conclusions in general. In a sense the play is a murder mystery in reverse: the *truth*, acted out in front of us, is discarded by the Judge (who is our stand-in for the detective of the murder mystery) and replaced by a distortion. It becomes the new, official 'truth' sanctioned by the Judge's position of authority. Prejudice masquerades as justice in the service of maintaining power.

While the 'action' of the play gives us all the evidence we need that the Judge's inquiry has been mistaken, it should be noted in what ways the Judge does not meet the standard of objectivity even with the information to which he has access.

- The Judge 'grills' the Policeman in his first scene about the presence of weapons on or near the corpses. The latter's constant response is that he was not the first to come upon the bodies. Though the Priest and the Photographer are interviewed, there is no evident attempt to find out who may really have been first to the bodies and have him or her give testimony.
- He accepts the testimony of Dr Winbourne without applying Professor Cuppley's testimony to it. Surely the incredible damage done by the soldiers' SLRs would make Dr Winbourne's assertions (about the smear marks and patterns of lead powder distribution) unsupportable.
- He allows himself the incorrect extrapolation, already discussed (see Scene 12, p.26), that because Skinner, Lily and Michael created some very minor mischief in the parlour they must have been planning to occupy it all along.
- His symbolic interpretation of these 'facts' clearly violates the 'objective' view he has been charged with creating.

The Judge's final remarks (p.168) contain some other misrepresentations:

- He blames the speakers for inciting the mob to violence, but we are meant to understand that the soldiers moved in before any violence occurred.
- He says 'there is no reason to assume that the soldiers would have opened fire if they had not been fired upon first'. This is not the way a tribunal or court of law is supposed to work. One does not naturally assume that if a person acted violently they must have

been provoked. True legal procedure would demand *proof* that the three fired upon the soldiers first. The Judge's statement is something like a lawyer making the argument that if a man was killed there is no reason to assume that he did not deserve to be killed.

- He also claims that he must accept the expert testimony that at least Michael and Lily fired weapons. But we'll remember that Dr Winbourne never states conclusively that Lily fired a weapon, only Michael (in both cases he is obviously wrong). The Judge has assumed this on his own.

Though the prejudice of the Judge is clearly the most harmful, there is prejudice to be found elsewhere in *The Freedom of the City*. Think of the Priest railing about 'revolutionaries'. Think of Skinner and Michael. They are ostensibly on the same side, protesting for the same things, but look how neither can see the other for what he really is. Skinner, deriding Michael's political naivety, cannot admit how reasonable the latter's demands are. And Michael, as already stated, cannot admit the legitimacy of methods or motives differing from his own. Having branded Skinner a 'hooligan', he cannot see him as anything else. Again, Friel wants us to see that even people 'on the same side' are subject to the kind of prejudices that tear them apart and can destroy their cause.

Subjectivity and objectivity

Closely related to the above theme is that of objectivity and subjectivity. Two prominent characters, the Judge and Dr Dodds, talk about objectivity in different ways. The first assures us that his tribunal intends to come up with an objective version of the events surrounding the killing. We have already explored how deeply it fails in this.

Dr Dodds tells us about how a sense of objectivity by individuals in the subculture of poverty is required before political action is undertaken. Much of Dodds' lecture is about the crippling subjective view the poor cannot seem to escape. Why is so much importance being placed on this issue? It could be argued that Friel is commenting on the heterogeneity of the protesters. In a movement that contains Skinners, Michaels and Lilys, there can obviously be no single objective goal, no objective reality. Everyone protests for his or her *own* reasons.

They say that history is written by the winners. In the world of *The Freedom of the City*, 'objectivity' is determined by the dominant culture. There is something uncompromising in Dr Dodds' speech, sympathetic as it is to the plight of the poor. Harping on about their 'present-time orientation' and subjectivity, Dodds is holding up objectivity as some kind of shining virtue. There is a double standard at work here. Is anyone demanding that the rich live 'objectively'? Surely the one thing having money allows is utter subjectivity, the freedom to see things in an individual way, to act according to individual desires. Why is this then a fault in the poor? In Dodds' model we should see Lily's uncanny perception of her own world, or her illogical march for her son Declan, as deep character flaws; we should see Skinner's impulsiveness as dangerous behaviour. Perhaps this is one of the ways that the poor are always 'overcharged'. Judged as being inadequate in the eyes of the dominant culture, they must not be allowed to live their lives subjectively; they must see the objective truth of how inadequate they are.

The Judge makes a mockery of objectivity by showing how the 'truth' is what the powerful want it to be. Dr Dodds makes objectivity one more hoop that the poor must jump through, one more measure of their powerlessness. In a more general way, the play explores this theme in all the testimony given by its various characters. *The Freedom of the City* is a nexus of competing, subjective versions of its central event. Everyone thinks they command the objective truth, but all versions are individual and subject to 'agendas' and personal prejudice. By throwing all these subjective views into the same pot, Friel is telling us that 'objectivity' is an illusion, most pointedly in the political world.

Key point

Note how even Friel's dramatic techniques seem to underscore this theme. The many juxtapositions we have looked at – Dodds' first speech with the Woman's speech at the rally; the Balladeer's song with the pronouncements of the Judge; the Priest's message with the press conference; Dodds' second speech with the testimony of Brigadier Johnson-Hansbury – all embody the competition of subjective versions. In fact, each version obscures the truth about that day in the Guildhall.

Freedom

The play leads us to address the question: what is freedom? Surely this is another subjective issue. Won't everyone have a slightly different answer? Perhaps so, but it is just as likely that we would agree on certain things. For instance, isn't Freedom (with a capital 'F') made up of many individual freedoms? Could we say that individuals are free if they are allowed to work where they want and say what they want, but are not allowed to follow their religious preferences, or to own property? No. We who live in the 'free world' know, or should know, that Freedom (capital 'F') is an abstract structure constructed of many tangible bricks. Knock one out and the whole structure collapses. We are not 'Free' unless we possess all those individual freedoms. This is of obvious importance to the play.

Skinner and Freedom

Think of all of Skinner's speeches about the 'freedom of the city'. (See comments in 'Scene-by-Scene Analysis' on Skinner's approach to the issue.) He tries to reduce it all to a joke in his 'defensive flippancy', but it is apparent that Skinner is troubled and angry. He may travel to Scotland, and he may put his money on the horses when he has it, but he is not free. How do we know? Well, the soldiers prove it with their bullets and the Judge proves it with his conclusions. One of the things Skinner means when he says 'the poor are always overcharged' has to do with freedom.

Because of his status as a poor man of 'no fixed address', Skinner is without political agency; he has no clout, no status in the world. In a word, he, along with Lily and Michael, is expendable.

Michael and Freedom

Now Michael, if he were asked, would say that he is free. He is free to look for work that never comes, free to take his night classes, free to join the protest marches. He is an optimist. Michael's belief in the rightness of his form of protest mirrors this. His assertion of the necessity for dignity and decorum is really a declaration of freedom. Obviously Michael would not march if he thought he was not being denied basic rights. When he talks about his desire for 'fair play' and says 'we'll get it because it's something every man's entitled to and nothing can stop us getting what we're entitled to' (p.161), he is asserting his *freedom*, almost as though it were a universal law that people born free will eventually prevail over tyranny.

Is this law true? Well, not in this case. Think of Michael's revelation at the moment of his death; at first sure that some mistake has been made, he seems to realise just how little value the British place on his life. Surely he comes to see the truth of Skinner's words: 'you presumed, boy ... this is theirs, boy, and your very presence here is a sacrilege' (p.140). What use is a show of dignity and decorum against people who do not even deign to grant you the *capacity* for these qualities? How can you show them you are 'free' people if they deny your status as *people*? Think of the terms being applied to Skinner, Lily and Michael. The Judge and Brigadier Johnson-Hanbury call them 'terrorists' (p.134), and Soldier 1 calls them 'fucking yobbos' (p.117). These aren't happy grounds for dialogue. On this issue of freedom the play seems to side with Skinner and not with Michael. The same bullets that shatter Michael's optimistic belief in his natural dignity justify Skinner's sardonic take on the 'freedom of the city'.

Lily and Freedom

What about Lily? Is she free? Lily does not speak in abstract concepts, so it is hard to come to certain conclusions. However, there is no denying that the deck has been stacked against her. With her eleven children, her miserable husband and her harsh circumstances, she must surely be seen as the least free character in the play. Yet there is no evidence that she sees herself in this way. We should be careful of assuming a kind of sentimentality that promotes sloppy thinking. It would be easy to fall into the trap of seeing Lily as a transcendent figure, an ur-mother ('ur' means original), a self-sacrificing mother figure who puts aside her cares to look after her family and those, like Skinner and Michael, who come into her contact. This is not the case at all. Lily loves her son Declan, and she is incredibly resourceful, but these qualities do not allow her to transcend her reality. They hold up the light to show just how hideous it really is. Lily can laugh and she can avoid feeling sorry for herself. This bespeaks a freedom of mind, but she is still a victim to her circumstances. Friel wants us to see the many ways she is more constrained than either Skinner or Michael. While her humanity adds real sorrow to her fate, seeing her as transcending her circumstances would devalue the bitterness of life for those like her.

Civic freedom

In discussing this theme, one must also consider the question of *civic* freedom. This issue is important if for no other reason than it gives the play its title. Two items to contrast are, firstly, the very brief shouts of the Woman who had been speaking at the rally as it is broken up by the troops: 'Stand your ground! Don't move! Don't panic! This is your city! This is your city!' (p.111); and secondly, Skinner's flippant rehearsing of the 'freedom of the city' ceremony in the Mayor's parlour. These, as well as the council minutes Skinner reads, all underscore how the Catholics are 'foreign' in their own city. Again, the implication is that the mundane life of the city, of opera guilds and rugby clubs, has nothing to do with those like Skinner, Lily and Michael. They are inhabitants of a city, but not 'citizens'; they are not free men and women. The fight for rights is in a sense the fight for the city. Freedom means being allowed to take possession of the place you live in. The awful thing about prejudice is that it presumes to say 'you don't belong here' to people who may have always been there. This is the ultimate disenfranchisement. The murder of the three for occupying the Guildhall and the subsequent condemnation of them by the Judge are echoes of those brutal words: 'you don't belong here'. That the soldiers and the Judge come from over the Irish Sea just underscores the lack of freedom the three and their kind suffer. They are strangers in their own city, and this is the greatest insult against freedom.

Protest marches – reasons for Catholic protest

We should have a closer look at what Skinner, Lily and Michael are protesting about and why their reasons for doing it are so different. There has been much academic debate about the extent of discrimination in the period from the founding of the nation of Northern Ireland until the beginning of the civil rights movement in 1968. Some say it was not nearly as bad as Catholic agitators have painted it. But most commentators agree that there certainly was discrimination. Of course discrimination, like beauty, is in the eye of the beholder; surely there would have been no civil rights movement if Catholics had felt they were receiving full civil rights.

There is most evidence of discrimination in areas like electoral practices, public employment and public housing. 'Gerrymandering' (manipulating electoral boundaries for political advantage) was seen as one of the most common tools employed by the Unionists for maintaining their hold on power. Electoral districts were manipulated in such a way that the Unionists came out with more representation, even if the majority of the population in that area was Catholic. It was also charged that only Unionists received good public service jobs. Unemployment has always been very high in Northern Ireland, but it was extraordinarily high among Catholics in this period (think of Michael). Very limited housing was built in times of population inflation; the result was that Catholics, who were contributing most to the increase, often had to live in expensive temporary accommodation or in tenement style housing (think of Lily). This was done, of course, to control the electoral rolls and to make sure that the Unionists came out on top.

These are the charges that have been made. While the precise reasons are complex and need not be grasped in detail, discrimination has been clearly *demonstrated*. The important thing is that there was a strong enough feeling among Catholics to create a civil rights movement. It is also important to understand something else about this movement. The NICRA, a nonviolent organisation, was dedicated to gaining rights *within* Northern Ireland. The IRA, though it might share some sympathies with the NICRA, was entirely separate, with the main goal of ending British rule in Northern Ireland and reunifying with the Republic of Ireland. Without realising this, one might get the wrong impression of Skinner, Lily and Michael. When the Balladeer refers to them as fighters or martyrs for reunification, he is making untrue assumptions. They are marching for rights and nothing more. Their position on the question of reunification is never known; Friel takes great pains to avoid the issue.

Why is this so important? It's because one of the protesters killed on Bloody Sunday was indeed a member of a youth wing of the IRA. Witnesses say that this young man's body (his name was William Nash) was removed from the scene by British soldiers. When he was later examined, nail bombs – a common weapon of the IRA – were found in his pockets. Needless to say, witnesses also assert that the weapons were not there when they came to his aid.

Are Michael, Skinner and Lily 'terrorists'?

What Northern Ireland's Catholics have found most insulting about the Widgery inquiry into Bloody Sunday are its implications that the shooting victims were terrorists. Without question, the Judge in *The Freedom of the City* is trying to pin that label on Skinner, Michael and Lily. To everyone involved that means one thing – the violent IRA – and how ironic it is that the Judge and the Balladeer paint such a similar picture of the victims. But it is clear that the three have nothing to do with the IRA.

Remember that at the beginning of the play the Policeman confirms that though Skinner has been in trouble countless times, he is not a suspected terrorist (p.109), and we can safely assume he is the only candidate of the three. Dramatically, if the three main characters were represented as IRA terrorists, audiences would struggle to identify with them, and it would not fit in with Friel's political agenda. This further underscores how complicated the situation was in Northern Ireland at the time of the play's setting.

Why do Michael, Skinner and Lily march?

Some of the divisions within the protest movement (never mind those between NICRA and the IRA, or between the nominal IRA and the provisional IRA, or between Sinn Féin and the so-called 'Real IRA') are present in the ideological separation between Michael and Skinner.

Again, Michael is fairly straightforward. Believing firmly in the capitalist system, he is trying to improve himself, to get a job and get ahead. The civil rights movement, when successful, will give him 'the same chance as the next fella'. Thus he believes in a protest movement that crosses the social spectrum and that is based on dignity, lawfulness and decorum. He despises violence. In a word, you might say that Michael represents order – not the punitive order of the British and the RUC, but the order of civil and universal laws. The rights Michael is marching for are 'natural rights'.

Skinner would take up one of the final points Dr Dodds makes, that political change has little effect on the poor (p.163). No matter who is in charge, no matter who makes the rules, the poor stay poor. There cannot be rich without poor. Michael is not going to get his chance – he is deluding himself. He and Skinner and Lily will never have 'the freedom of the city' no matter who prevails. To Skinner, Michael's desire for order and control is both naive and destructive – naive because it will never work, and destructive because it keeps in place the apparatus of wealth that shuts out people like them. It is for this reason that Skinner leans towards anarchy; the whole system needs to be destroyed so that something else can begin. There is a violence to Skinner, but it is limited to his ideas rather than his actions. Perhaps this accounts for his frustration; without his evident sense of morality – as expressed in his speeches, primarily to Lily – Skinner might just be one of the killers. But this strays from the point. Skinner marches out of this sense of frustration, but also out of identification. He identifies with the poor (Michael included) who never get a fair share.

Who is correct? Well, it is no longer 1970, and while Northern Ireland is still subject to great political turmoil, prosperity is finding its way to both parts of Ireland. But is not the gap between rich and poor, haves and have-nots, widening around the world? The world is still full of Skinners who must live on their wits. And Northern Ireland remains partitioned. And many still feel disenfranchised, politically and economically.

And what about Lily's reason for marching? Her thinking is not politically motivated. Yet somehow her marching for her son Declan makes sense, even if it runs completely contrary to Dr Dodds' position that the extreme poor become political once they get an objective perspective of their plight, and that they march out of hope for themselves and for the people like them all over the world. There could not be a less objective reason for marching than Lily's. And there is no hope involved; if anything, it is done out of hopelessness. In this she is exactly opposite to Michael, though perhaps she is not so far from Skinner. Having lived a life of struggle and degradation, Lily finally finds the voice to protest the one awful thing she can do nothing about. We might call it an existential protest directed against the inherent unfairness of 'Life'. It lays so much trouble at the door of some and so little at the door of others. Perhaps having experienced something that cannot be remedied, Lily sees the vital importance of trying to change what one can.

Again, such interpretations do not necessarily illuminate things; Lily does not pretend her protest is logical, quite the reverse. The important thing is that she protests for reasons entirely her own. And she thus disproves the theories of people like the Judge and Dr Dodds and the Balladeer. Protest movements are composed of individuals with their own ideas, their own motivations, and their own desires. To lump them all together and to try to come up with a single reason for their actions is to deny them their identity as humans. In the end, *The Freedom of the City* is a play about humans.

QUESTIONS & ANSWERS

This section focuses on your own analytical writing on the text, and gives you strategies for producing high-quality responses in your coursework and exam essays.

Essay writing – an overview

An essay on a literary work is a formal and serious piece of writing that presents your point of view on the text, usually in response to a given topic. Your 'point of view' in an essay is your interpretation of the meaning of the text's language, structure, characters, situations and events, supported by detailed analysis of textual evidence.

Analyse – don't summarise

In your essays it is important to avoid simply summarising what happens in a text.

- A **summary** is a description or paraphrase (retelling in different words) of the characters and events. For example: 'Macbeth has a horrifying vision of a dagger dripping with blood before he goes to murder King Duncan.'
- An **analysis** is an explanation of the real meaning or significance that lies 'beneath' the text's words (and images, for a film). For example: 'Macbeth's vision of a bloody dagger shows how deeply uneasy he is about the violent act he is contemplating, and conveys his sense that supernatural forces are impelling him to act.'

A limited amount of summary is sometimes necessary to let your reader know which part of the text you wish to discuss. However, always keep this to a minimum and follow it immediately with your analysis of what this part of the text is really telling us.

Plan your essay

Carefully plan your essay so that you have a clear idea of what you are going to say. The plan ensures that your ideas flow logically, that your argument remains consistent and that you stay on the topic. An essay plan should be a list of **brief dot points** – no more than half a page.

Include your central argument or main contention – a concise statement (usually in a single sentence) of your overall response to the topic. See 'Analysing a Sample Topic' for guidelines on how to formulate a main contention.

Write three or four dot points for each paragraph indicating the main idea and evidence/examples from the text. Note that in your essay you will need to *expand* on these points and *analyse* the evidence.

Structure your essay

An essay is a complete, self-contained piece of writing. It has a clear beginning (the introduction), middle (several body paragraphs) and end (the last paragraph or conclusion). It must also have a central argument that runs throughout, linking each paragraph to form a coherent whole. See examples of introductions and conclusions in the 'Analysing a Sample Topic' and 'Sample Answer' sections.

The introduction establishes your overall response to the topic. It includes your main contention and outlines the main evidence you will refer to in the course of the essay. Write your introduction *after* you have done a plan and *before* you write the rest of the essay.

The body paragraphs argue your case – they present evidence from the text and explain how this evidence supports your argument. Each body paragraph needs:

- a strong **topic sentence** (usually the first sentence) that states the main point being made in the paragraph
- **evidence** from the text, including some brief quotations
- **analysis** of the textual evidence, with explanation of its significance and how it supports your argument
- **links back to the topic** in one or more statements, usually towards the end of the paragraph.

Connect the body paragraphs so that your discussion flows smoothly. Use some linking words and phrases such as 'similarly' and 'on the other hand', though don't start every paragraph like this. Another strategy is to use a significant word from the last sentence of one paragraph in the first sentence of the next.

Use key terms from the topic – or synonyms for them – throughout, so the relevance of your discussion to the topic is always clear.

The conclusion ties everything together and finishes the essay. It includes strong statements that emphasise your central argument and provide a clear response to the topic.

Avoid simply restating the points made earlier in the essay – this will end on a very flat note and imply that you have run out of ideas and vocabulary. The conclusion should be a logical extension of what you have written, not just a repetition or summary of it. Writing an effective conclusion can be a challenge. Try using these tips:

- Start by linking back to the final sentence of the second-last paragraph – this helps your writing to flow, rather than leaping back to your main contention straight away.
- Use synonyms and expressions with equivalent meanings to vary your vocabulary. This allows you to reinforce your line of argument without being repetitive.
- When planning your essay, think of one or two broad statements or observations about the text's wider meaning. These should be related to the topic and your overall argument. Keep them for the conclusion, since they will give you something 'new' to say but still follow logically from your discussion. The introduction will be focused on the topic, but the conclusion can present a wider view of the text.

Essay topics

1. Skinner says to Michael: "Because you presumed, boy. Because this is theirs, boy, and your very presence here is a sacrilege."
'Skinner shows that he understands, far better than Michael, the danger of the situation for the trio in the Guildhall.' Do you agree?

2. 'The Judge establishes himself as just that – a judge who condemns three innocent people.' How do *you* judge the Judge?

3. "You and him and everybody else marching and protesting about sensible things like politics and stuff and me in the middle of you all, marching for Declan. Isn't that the stupidest thing you ever heard?"
What does this reveal to us about Lily's character?

4. 'Brian Friel creates sympathy for Michael, Skinner and Lily because he structures events in such a way that we see that the three are innocent.' Discuss.

5. 'There are two crucial settings in *The Freedom of the City* – Derry and the Guildhall.' How does Friel use these settings to help the audience understand the dilemmas that Michael, Lily and Skinner face?

6. Discuss some of the staging choices Friel makes in this play and how they help you to understand two important characters.

7. Consider the Judge's stated mission: "Our only function is to form an objective view of the events which occurred in the city of Londonderry on the 10th day of February 1970".
Is this mission fulfilled?

8. 'It is their occupation of the Mayor's parlour in the Derry Guildhall that really leads to the deaths and later condemnation of Lily, Michael and Skinner.' Discuss.

9. "MICHAEL: And that was really impressive – all those people marching along in silence, rich and poor, high and low, doctors, accountants, plumbers, teachers, bricklayers … knowing that what they wanted was their rights.
SKINNER: It has nothing to do with doctors and accountants and teachers and dignity and boy scout honour. It's about us – the poor – the majority – stirring in our sleep."
Who does Friel show is right – Michael or Skinner?

10 "WOMAN: Stand your ground! Don't move! Don't panic! This is your city! This is your city!"
Is Derry Skinner, Lily and Michael's city?

11 'The Balladeer, the Priest and the Judge are all critical in revealing the powerlessness of the poor.' Discuss.

12 '*The Freedom of the City* demonstrates that the voices of power are pitted against the voices of powerlessness.' Discuss.

13 'Dr Dodds' theories about the subculture of poverty effectively highlight that the real issue of poverty is being completely ignored in the Tribunal's inquiry.' Do you agree?

14 'In *The Freedom of the City*, Friel shows that justice is impossible to achieve because of the political prejudice.' Discuss.

Analysing a sample topic

Discuss the symbolic significance of the three protagonists' occupation of the Mayor's parlour in the Derry Guildhall.

- The question is asking you to look at **symbolic** importance. A symbol is an object that has political or emotional meaning beyond its function. Thus you are being asked to look at the political or emotional value that characters in the play place on the Guildhall.
- Think about the play's major characters. Which ones are particularly interested in what the Guildhall stands for? Certainly Skinner, Lily and Michael are, considering that they are trapped inside it. The Judge is also very interested, especially as he is trying to determine the motives of the three in entering it in the first place. Others, like the Balladeer and Liam O'Kelly, mention the significance of this place as well.
- Choose which characters you will discuss. Narrow your choices to two or three – it is better to discuss these in depth than to skim over all of them. Further, choose characters with opposing views, as this will give you more opportunities for discussion. The richest characters in this regard could be Skinner and the Judge. There is nothing wrong

with saying something about each character's perspective, but write the bulk of the essay on Skinner and the Judge.

- Having chosen characters with opposite views, it is necessary to contrast their approaches in your essay. In order to do this you must understand fully just where each one stands on the issue. Write a statement of two or three sentences concerning the position of each – focus on getting your ideas clear at this stage.
- Try to find lines from the play that support your conclusions. Hint: While Skinner talks about the parlour on many occasions, there is likely to be something valuable in his early speeches. You may also remember that the Judge, in his first speech in Act Two, comes to a conclusion about the intentions of the three having to do exactly with the symbolic significance of the Guildhall. Make sure to quote these lines in your essay.
- Before writing, consider that the opinions of Skinner and the Judge represent their entire way of thinking. Their thoughts on this topic are consistent with their larger philosophies. It is appropriate to discuss these philosophies, as long as you link the discussion to the issue the question addresses. Certainly many of Skinner's ideas could be applied to this topic.
- In writing a comparison/contrast essay, it is best to make your points about one character in bulk before moving onto the other character. Jumping back and forth between the two subjects can lead to confusion in your writing.
- As you write about each character, it is appropriate to compare and contrast them briefly with other characters. For example, it might illuminate your discussion about Skinner to contrast his symbolic understanding to Michael's, say, or the Balladeer's. It is not then necessary to contrast these opinions to those of the Judge.
- While it is important to fully address the topic itself, questions like this are always designed to give you an opportunity to show that you understand the text in question. Take the opportunity; show the examiners that you can relate their question to the important themes and issues of the play.

SAMPLE ANSWER

'Language can be an avenue for revealing the truth and it can be used as a way of evading reality.' How does the play show this to be true?

Language is a powerful tool for individuals or groups in times of political unrest. Brian Friel's *The Freedom of the City* demonstrates this truth eloquently. While the sympathies of the play seem to be firmly lodged with the peaceful protestors against British oppression in Northern Ireland, no side is entirely spared from Friel's condemnation. Members of the British authority, protestors, news reporters, academics and priests are all revealed, by the language they use, to be self-serving political creatures. One of the play's messages is that language creates its own reality, whether it is used in a genuine attempt to describe the truth or deployed to create lies and deception.

There is no better literary form than theatre to demonstrate the power of language to reveal truth or evade reality. Without the benefit of the descriptive passages in prose narratives, audience members or readers of plays have only the dialogue (and to a lesser extent the actions) of characters to judge them by. Although Michael, Skinner and Lily use language in interesting ways to create individual realities for themselves, the purposeful use of language to create a specific reality is more evident in the dialogue of the secondary characters. The Judge, the Priest, the Balladeer and Liam O'Kelly each represent a particular occupation which is engaged in the political crisis. It is not surprising that Brian Friel does not strongly develop any of these characters beyond the functions they serve in their occupations and on behalf of their political masters.

The Judge is the worst offender against the truth. Though he says the 'right' things about impartiality and looking objectively at the facts in his introduction to the inquest, it soon becomes clear that his tribunal has no interest in finding out the truth. He leads witnesses, and he doesn't interview anyone who might offer an alternative version of the events to that espoused by the British army. In the end he pronounces judgement on the trio in the Guildhall based on extremely dubious evidence. But the language he uses suggests that his tribunal has been a model of propriety. Intent on maintaining the status quo, the Judge uses the language of power and authority to convince his listeners, and no doubt himself, that he is impartial, and that his conclusions are correct.

On the opposite side of the political divide is the Balladeer. The difference between these two characters is made even stronger when the type of speech they use is contrasted. The Judge uses the dry language of the court while the Balladeer uses the bawdy rhymes of his street songs. But the Balladeer's account of the true motives of Michael, Skinner and Lily is just as inaccurate as the Judge's. In the Balladeer's version the three are militant heroes and martyrs sacrificing themselves for the cause of reunification. The audience, who gain a strong understanding of the motives and values of the central characters, understand that the 'reality' constructed by the Balladeer bears little relationship to the truth.

The Priest uses the deaths of Michael, Skinner and Lily to launch into a political diatribe against communism. He paints them as Christian heroes fighting godlessness. While this is completely inaccurate, it is the reality that the Priest would like to be true. He is prepared to promulgate it whether he genuinely believes it or not. Friel shows that political desire can corrupt even those who are supposed to be invulnerable to corruption – their language is the way they reveal themselves, as well as the means by which they seek to impose their views on others.

Liam O'Kelly is the news presenter reporting on the situation in the Guildhall for a television station in Ireland. Not bothering to get his facts straight, O'Kelly is eager to blow a minor incident into a crisis. Through O'Kelly's character and language use, Friel is commenting on the power of the media to inflame situations and to direct public opinion, a quality to be condemned in an occupation that requires balance and impartiality. In many ways, the reality O'Kelly tries to create actually becomes true. His report that 'fifty armed gunmen have taken possession of the Guildhall' helps to create the tense atmosphere that ends in the murder of the three main characters.

Through the juxtaposition of conflicting versions of the same events, Friel shows the difficulty of establishing a relationship between language and truth when powerful forces are in violent conflict. Expert witnesses are brought in to offer forensic evidence on the conditions of the bodies and the presence of lead particles. However, in the Judge's inquest, all this testimony – however objective and scientific it appears – is directed at creating a reality that has nothing to do with the truth. Yet it is a reality that is given force and legitimacy by the power of the court and the authority of the Judge. *The Freedom of the City* shows that reality can be shaped by language, and that language can be used by those with political interests both to present the 'truth' and to evade reality. Those who have political power ultimately control both language and reality, regardless of the truth.

REFERENCES & READING

Text

Friel, Brian, *Plays: 1*, Faber, London, 1996.

Further reading

Andrews, Elmer, *The Art of Brian Friel: Neither Reality Nor Dreams*, MacMillan, London, 1995.

Connolly, S.J. (ed), *The Oxford Companion to Irish History*, Oxford University Press, Oxford, 1998.

Dantanus, Ulf, *Brian Friel: The Growth of an Irish Dramatist*, Acta Universitas Gothoburgiensis, Gothenburg, 1985.

Deane, Seamus, Introduction to *Plays: 1* (Brian Friel), Faber, London, 1996.

Deane, Seamus, *The Field Day Anthology of Irish Writing*, Field Day, Derry, 1991.

Kiberd, Declan, *Inventing Ireland*, Harvard Univ. Press, Cambridge MA, 1996.

McClean, Raymond, *The Road to Bloody Sunday*, Guildhall Press, Derry, 1987. For excerpts, see http://cain.ulst.ac.uk/events/bsunday/mcclean.htm

Peacock, Alan, ed. *The Achievement of Brian Friel*, Colin Smyth, Gerrads Cross, 1993.

Pine, Richard, *Brian Friel and Ireland's Drama*, Routledge, London, 1990.

Whyte, John, 'How much discrimination was there under the Unionist regime, 1921-1968?', in *Contemporary Irish Studies*, eds Tom Gallagher & James O'Connell, Manchester Univ. Press, Manchester, 1983, http://cain.ulst.ac.uk/issues/discrimination/whyte.htm

GLOSSARY OF TERMS – IRISH CONTEXTS

Anglo-Irish Treaty (1921) – An agreement between the British government and Irish negotiators leading to the establishment of two countries: the Irish Free State (eventually called the Republic of Ireland), and Northern Ireland.

Bloody Sunday – The circumstances of *The Freedom of the City* are most likely based on the events of 30 January 1972, known as Bloody Sunday. On this day British paratroopers shot thirteen Catholic protesters dead when they were sent to make arrests after a protest march was banned in Derry (the fourteenth person died six months later). This led to greatly increased violence, which in turn led to direct rule of Northern Ireland from London.

Bogside – A suburban area in Derry, with predominantly working-class, Catholic/Republican residents.

Catholics (in Ireland) – The Republic of Ireland is overwhelmingly a Catholic nation, but in Northern Ireland Catholics are in the minority (the majority is Protestant).

Derry – Officially named Londonderry, the city was founded on the old town of Derry, the name by which it is still known to Catholics. It is Northern Ireland's second largest city after Belfast.

Home Rule – A political arrangement where a region is permitted a large degree of autonomy. The movement in Ireland concerned when government of Ireland would be returned from the British to the Irish.

internment – The policy of detaining suspected paramilitary personnel without trial, initiated by the Unionist Northern Ireland government in 1971.

IRA (Irish Republican Army) – Originally formed early in the twentieth century, this group fought violently for Home Rule against England. After this was achieved, the IRA went dormant until the 1960s when it began agitating for reunification of the two countries. In 1969 a major split led to the Official IRA (which generally supports political action to achieve Irish unity) and the Provisional IRA. The latter, having renamed itself as the 'Real IRA' in the late 1990s, is the dominant republican terrorist force today – responsible for the shootings and bombings in Northern Ireland, Britain and Europe.

Loyalist – An individual or group (usually Protestant) in Northern Ireland who is loyal to Great Britain. Also called *Unionist.*

Nationalist – An individual or group (usually Catholic) in favour of Irish independence from Great Britain. Also called *Republican.*

NICRA (Northern Ireland Civil Rights Association) – Formed in Belfast in 1967, the civil rights group included liberals, trade unionists, communists and republicans. It drew its inspiration from the success of Martin Luther King in the USA and the British-based National Council for Civil Liberties. NICRA became significantly active in 1968 and made international news when television showed the unjustifiably violent response to a march in Derry on 5 October 1968 and on Bloody Sunday in 1972.

Northern Ireland – One of the nations of the United Kingdom, it was formed from six of Ireland's original thirty-two counties after the Anglo-Irish Treaty.

Orange Brigades/Orange Order/Orangemen – Names for terrorist and non-terrorist political groups supporting the Protestant/Unionist cause in Northern Ireland. 'Orange' comes from William of Orange, the great champion of the Protestants who defeated the Catholic James II at the Battle of the Boyne in 1690.

partitioned – A term describing the segregation of a city or country along ethnic, religious or political lines.

Protestants (in Ireland) – Protestantism is a branch of Christianity, originating in the sixteenth century Reformation when it split away from the Roman Catholic Church. Northern Ireland is dominated by a Protestant majority.

Republic of Ireland – The nation formed by the twenty-six Catholic counties of Ireland after the Anglo-Irish Treaty. It was a member of the Commonwealth until the 1940s, but is now wholly independent.

Republican – An individual or group (usually Catholic) who supports the removal of British sovereignty from Northern Ireland. Also called *Nationalist.*

RUC (Royal Ulster Constabulary) – The police force of Northern Ireland, formed in 1922. It was originally intended that thirty per cent of the RUC should be Catholics but by 1970 only about ten per cent were Catholics. Consequently, Catholics regarded this force as serving Unionist (Protestant) interests.

Sinn Féin – A republican political party active in Ireland and Northern Ireland, founded in 1905. It took its current form in 1970 after a split within the party. Its name is Irish for 'we ourselves'.

The Taoiseach (Prime Minister) – The Head of Government in the Republic of Ireland.

The Troubles – This term first came into use early in the twentieth century to refer to any of the violence or social strife resulting from the Republican struggle against the British. Today it is used to refer to the sectarian violence in Northern Ireland.

Ulster – The name of the region (historically, a kingdom) that comprises the six counties of Northern Ireland.

Unionist – Advocators (usually Protestant) who support retaining the political union between Great Britain and Northern Ireland. Also called *Loyalist.*